FPL 3

Kelly 

Always Seeing, Never Speaking

Always Seeing, Never Speaking:

The Testimony of a Seer

By

Kelly J. Caselman

ISBN: 978-1-7336960-5-0

DEDICATION

To my family, Kara, Alexandra, Mikayla, and Logan. Both *grace* and *forgiveness* are very powerful words. Never let us forget that we all have the ability to glance in the rearview mirror of our lives, but it is the windshield before us that God uses to direct our futures with him.

Contents

Introduction

In my first book, *Through the Eyes of a Seer*, I talked about the Old Testament and New Testament seers and prophets and wondered about the origination of their "gifts" and the struggles that they went through. I asked about great men of the Bible, such as Peter, Paul, and Stephen, and what it would have been like if they had been silenced by society. I suppose that Paul and Stephen were silenced, as their lives ended with martyrs' deaths, but not until God's word had been spread for many years through them and they had raised up numerous believers to carry on the work of the church—Paul being the one who wrote most of the New Testament books.

My life as a seer has been filled with wonder and heartache. But my job as a seer, to be a perceiver of hidden truth, is a spiritual battle—one that takes discipline and a great deal of prayer to discern how and when God wants me to present the truth. God is so gracious in his words and dealings with us.

There is a lot of misinformation and misconception about the spiritual realm. It is conveyed as a frightening and uncontrollable world. This is simply not true, I know, as someone who has been able to see into it since I was a young child. God sent his Son, Jesus, to redeem us and give us the right and authority to speak and pray directly to him, to use Jesus's name as the name above all names. In his name there is power, as it says in Philippians 2:9–11 (NLT): "Therefore, God elevated him to the place of highest honor and gave him the name above all other names, that at the name of Jesus every knee shall bow, in heaven and on earth and under the earth, and every tongue declare that Jesus Christ is Lord, to the glory of God the Father."

It is important to reiterate that life is a real struggle that we all deal with, and the only way to truly live victoriously and defeat the agents of the enemy when they come against us is by the name of Jesus.

Chapter 1: Seeing into the Past

Stationed in West Germany in the mid-1980s, I found myself surrounded by so many people—people who would tell you we were good friends, both military coworkers as well as civilians. The truth was they only knew a part of me, the part that I allowed them to know, and the other half I wasn't allowed to reveal; I was still unsure of what people would say about my imaginary friends or my gift. The angelic entity that had visited me earlier spoke of the path that had been set before me, and even though I was given the gift of seeing in the spirit, at times I felt like a blind man wandering throughout this world with very little direction as to the actual reason why I was given this gift.

As my potential date of separation or date of reenlistment from the military began to close in, I was asked to make a decision pertaining to my future. I decided to move forward as before, one day at a time. After I had spent six months in a burn unit in Germany, they were still reluctant to send me back to my unit, and the thought of going back to my original job, which was a maintenance position, I viewed as a step down from what I had been doing for the last several years. I still enjoyed traveling around Europe, and sometime earlier I had been introduced by a female friend of mine (who could also see in the spirit) to a tour guide in Rome,

Italy. The tour guide understood that I had the ability to see in the spirit and wanted to get my perspective on some tours that his agency had picked up the rights to start booking. He said that it seemed spooky in his opinion, and before he started trekking around as a guide in this area, he wanted my opinion as to just what he was getting himself into.

Taking a bus down to Rome, I was without a doubt excited to find out where it was we would be going. As I got off the bus in Rome, my new friend was there waiting with a sign in his hand; unfortunately, it was in Italian, and I couldn't read it, but according to him, it said something about not being afraid of any ghosts. I'm sure it had some reference to a movie that had been released years earlier. Getting into his car, he was very excited and told me that we were going to be visiting some catacombs under the city of Rome. He knew that where I grew up in Southern California, there were also catacombs that I had explored and was curious to find out if my results would be the same in Rome.

We parked his car and started walking down a brick path. He said this was a very famous area in Rome called the Appian Way where many tombs and Roman monuments were found, and many of Rome's wealthy found their final resting places along this stretch of highway. But the early

Christians were not buried among Rome's elite; the early Christians who did not believe in cremation were buried in the catacombs under the streets of the Appian Way. In the catacombs were thousands of Christians as well as martyrs and saints. As we entered into this underground labyrinth equipped with only large flashlights, my friend stated, "As soon as you start seeing things in the other realm, let me know."

I smiled and said, "You will be the first."

I asked him if we could turn off our flashlights for a minute. He said, "Only if I can put my hand on your shoulder, so I know you're not going to leave me." So he did.

My eyes were struggling to adjust; there was very little light, and I could almost feel an entity of fear trying to whisper thoughts into my mind quietly. I bound those thoughts in Jesus's name. I asked my friend to turn on his flashlight but to aim it at our feet so there would be as little light as possible in front of me. He said, "Well, that works for me; some light is better than no light at all."

I felt in my heart that this deception, this demon of fear, was only here because of the darkness, and just then my hunch was proven to be correct: my eyes began to fix on a dim light down one of the corridors. I asked my friend, "Do you see that light?"

He responded, "There is no light in that hallway; all I see is darkness."

I instructed him to keep the flashlight at his feet and let me follow the light that I was seeing. Light in my mind only meant one thing: angelic entities. As I followed, it began to get brighter. The light wasn't moving but was staying in one place, and as I got closer, I realized that there were many lights in these catacombs. Angels started to appear to me—not hundreds or thousands, but maybe a dozen or so—and as more of them appeared, I started to walk into what my friend felt was darkness. He asked, "How do you know your way, and how do you know we won't get lost?"

I told him, "First of all, the angels will show me the way, and they will not allow me to become lost. Second, God's word says, 'His word is a lamp for my feet, a light on my path' [Ps. 119:105, NIV]."

Not a word was spoken to me from these angelic beings, but each one acknowledged that I was able to see them as well as they could see me. A few of them smiled due to my friend dragging around this entity of fear with him, combined with the hopes that these ministering spirits could show me the way out. I asked him if he could loosen his grip on my shoulder because I was losing feeling in my right hand, so he let go of my shoulder and just grabbed a handful of my shirt. He said, "Buddy, I'd be lying if I told you I wasn't a little bit afraid."

I told him, "I am well aware of your fear, and so are the angelic beings, but in Jesus's name, I cast out that spirit of fear. Have faith!"

In these catacombs there were slots in the walls where families of the deceased would place their loved ones' remains. They were four to six slots high; in many of these slots were the bones of some of the deceased. I couldn't help but wonder about their stories and what they must have endured for their Christian faith. Some of the cutouts were shaped like arches, and others were recessed back into the walls as to be slightly separated from the others. Maybe this is where some of the early saints and martyrs would have found their final resting places. The angelic entities that I was allowed to see significantly congregated in these areas. Oddly enough, in this space, I was able to cast off the spirit of fear, and I felt nothing but peace—like I was in a place of worship, a place where I could almost feel God's presence. I have no doubt there were many prayers lifted up from this underground labyrinth of graves, and I turned to my friend and said, "There's nothing to fear here. There is only peace from my early brothers and sisters in Christ."

It was strange that in a place so dirty and dusty that only by God allowing me to see into the spirit was the light able to be detected. In this place, except for the shuffling of our feet as we walked along the dirt paths, it was silent. I could almost hear the early Christians mourning over their loved ones yet full of faith that in heaven they would have eternity together. I felt in my heart that someday I would get to meet these early Christians who walked the earth thousands of years ago, but instead of it being in these catacombs, it would be on the streets of gold in a heavenly kingdom.

Continuing to walk, I began to realize that there were areas in which I was unable to see the glows of angelic presence. At first, I wasn't sure if it was me or if I was entering an area where true darkness existed. My friend asked if I felt the temperature beginning to drop. It was very cool in the catacombs, but in this new passageway, it seemed to be even cooler. I, too, wanted to turn on my flashlight, but I decided to leave it off and prayed softly under my breath instead. Not wanting to allow fear to enter in, we kept moving forward. My friend asked if we had taken a wrong turn. I said, "No, I just want to see what was down this way."

He asked, "Did the angelic entities lead you in this direction?"

I said, "No, I was just curious."

He responded, "The way I understand, it's curiosity that killed the cat."

I replied, “Jesus said that all authority in heaven and on earth has been given to me.” (This is from Matthew 28:18, NIV.)

With that I started seeing dark shadows moving across the paths in front of me, some moving across the walls. Just then I stopped. My friend asked what was wrong, and I told him to trust me. I explained to him again that I see both sides of the spiritual realm. You cannot see one half without seeing the other half. In this domain they are both present, and we have a choice as to which one we follow.

He said, “I vote we follow the shiny ones.”

I said, “I agree, but I know and they know that in Jesus’s name, I have authority over them.”

In truth, right or wrong, sometimes I just wanted to see what their game plan was. I knew that I played from the standpoint of victory.

What had appeared to me in the spirit were several smaller demonic entities as well as one larger one standing among them wearing a hood like a fifth-century executioner.

I told myself, “You know this is just a manifestation, and in Jesus’s name, I will not allow fear to enter into my mind.”

Softly, I said, “In Jesus’s name, appear to me as you truly are and not in the form of the lie that you are showing me.”

Slowly, he shrank down into the same size as other demonic entities. Still quietly praying, I started to walk forward into the area they inhabited when I felt something pulling me backward, almost knocking me off my feet. This was something I hadn't encountered before; then I heard my friend's voice saying, "I don't know where you think you're going, but unless it's out of here, you aren't going anywhere."

As I regained my balance, I noticed that the demonic entities had moved in extremely close. It was when my friend pulled me backward; it must have created a moment of fear in me when I didn't know what was happening, and that was all they needed to move in much closer.

I spoke in a normal tone but with a sense of sternness, "In Jesus's name I cast you out of this place. You will have no authority here!"

My friend asked, "They are here, aren't they?"

I told him, "They were here, but they're gone now."

He asked, "You kicked spiritual rear end down here, didn't you?"

I said, "Nope. I was just exercising my spiritual authority in Jesus's name."

It appeared that somehow, we had made our way from early Christian burial sites into the areas where the occult may have performed ancient rituals. This section of the catacombs felt more familiar to me, like what I was used to seeing in the catacombs under the house where I lived in Southern California. Continuing to pray softly under my breath, I wanted to stay casting the demonic entities out, and in some ways it brought back thoughts from my childhood. I knew that as long as I didn't let them take control of the battlefield in my mind, I would be just fine. Unfortunately, I didn't take into account the guy walking behind me who by this point, was about to rip the sleeve off my shirt.

He blabbed, "You're a lousy tour guide."

And with that he took my flashlight and turned them both on, constantly waving them behind us as if there were somebody following us.

He said, "I have to admit, I'm starting to freak out just a little bit. Is there any chance you know the way out of here? Maybe you can petition your shiny friends to show us a speedy way out."

With that he started aiming the flashlights in every direction. We vaguely looked like a broken lighthouse on the ocean with lights shining in every direction, as if to warn ships not to come this way. I told him to give me a minute to get my bearings, and quietly I asked the Lord to show me a way out. Almost as fast as I got the words out of my mouth, I saw a dim light. I told my friend, "Let's walk this way."

He said, “Anyplace is better than were we are standing right now.”

As we began to walk, there were several areas where we found steps of only four or five at a time, but we were moving up hill. After some time, the darkness began to go away, and it was replaced with the dim lights that I had been following earlier on in the catacombs. The heaviness had left us, and once again I felt as if we were surrounded by God’s light. My friend mentioned that walking was good. He liked movement, and after being down in this underground graveyard walking for hours, my friend realized that these ministering spirits had brought us back to the place where we had entered. He thought it was absolutely amazing. I said to him, “What you call amazing, I call walking in faith.”

I told him the first thing he needed to tell his groups when they come into these underground Christian cemeteries is that there is nothing to fear here, and unless you allow fear to enter in, it has no place. Deception will try to do what people have allowed it to do for centuries—to deceive us into thinking there is something there when there is not. More often than not, fear is in our mind, and the word says, “Casting down imaginations, and every high thing that exalteth itself against the knowledge of God, and bringing into captivity every thought to the obedience of Christ” (2 Cor. 10:5, KJV), so that we may not fall into deception.

When we finally came out of the catacombs, the light of day almost felt strange, and it took a few minutes for our eyes to adjust. The dim light that I was allowed to see in the catacombs was there so that I might know what it took to perpetuate the word of God, and more often than not, it meant giving our lives for what we believe in.

Walking back to his car down this ancient street, my friend conveyed that tomorrow, we were going to go to someplace a lot less spooky.

I said, “Let’s face it, my friend. In Rome everything has a dark past, and besides that, I have been to many places throughout Europe that were just fine on the surface and in the spirit, it was far from God’s presence.”

He revealed that on the trip the following day, we would be going to different parts of the Vatican that his agency had acquired permission to see. He thought it would be fun if he gave me a test run of his tour, and of course seeing parts of the Vatican that I had previously not seen sounded like an incredible day. I couldn’t wait for tomorrow.

The hotel that I booked in Rome was a nice hotel and newly renovated, but from the look of the building, it was by no means new. I have always tried to make it a point to pray over my hotel room before going to sleep; call it a type of spiritual housekeeping. In the past I had been in hotel rooms where I had felt a dark presence and couldn’t put my finger on why it was there, so briefly praying over it has always allowed me to sleep just a little bit better.

The next day when my friend picked me up from the hotel, he said that we would have to go over to his place of employment and get some paperwork in order as well as his tour-guide credentials so that we would be allowed to go into certain parts of the Vatican. The Vatican is a city-state within a city, so in some ways, it's like going into a different country. After going through some checkpoints, we entered in through Saint Peter's Square. Before we got to the building, I stopped and was looking at the architecture. My friend said, "You have seen this many times; has something caught your attention that you haven't seen before?"

I told him that I had never really looked, but I wasn't aware that there was what looked like small gargoyles on the upper parts of the structure. He said they weren't gargoyles but 140 statutes that depict popes, martyrs, evangelists, and other religious figures. I told him that I knew what the statues are but, on the underside, down near the pillars I saw what looked to be gargoyles. He said, "I think you're crazy. Or is it possible you're seeing things that the rest of us are not?"

I asked him if it would be OK if we stayed there for a few minutes so that I could try to figure out what it was that I was seeing; because he didn't see it, I had to assume that I was seeing in the spirit. After about fifteen or twenty minutes, I realized that these gargoyle-looking entities were only under a few of the statues, so I asked my tour-guide friend about those particular statues. He said that all of the statues that I had pointed out were some of the different popes, and those particular ones had a rather shady past or short time as pope. What I was seeing were not gargoyles but demonic entities that would move ever so slightly, trying not to reveal themselves to the people who were not able to see them in the spirit. My friend asked me if I was satisfied and if we could go into the building now. I said, "Yep, I just wanted to know what it was I was looking at on the outside of the building."

I was even more intrigued about what we would come across inside these walls. As we entered what I know as the Vatican Museum, my friend said he wanted to take me first to Borgia Tower, where there were some rooms that used to be apartments for one of the popes. As we walked, we saw the beautiful paintings and arched ceilings found throughout beautiful Vatican City, but once my eyes moved past the beauty that I could see in the natural, I began to see in that parallel plane of the supernatural. It started out as faint whispers so quiet I could barely make out the words. There was unrest and pain; there was death in this room, and in the spiritual, I could see pools of blood and splatters on the walls. I could hear groans of people dying, and my friend asked me if I was OK, but I could only hear his voice in the background of my mind. What I was fixated on was the pain of events that had been experienced in this very room. Now I understood why this room had been sealed off for such a long period of time. I am sure that I was not the only one who knew what had taken place in these chambers. The only thing I knew to do was to pray softly and ask God to bring peace to this particular set of rooms.

My friend asked me to follow him into the hall of the Sibyls; he said, "When you get quiet like that, it makes me thankful that I don't have the same spiritual gifts that you have."

As we walked into the beautiful hall, I could sense death there as well; darkness was all around me. In some ways I wanted to understand what it was I was feeling and seeing in the spirit, but in other ways, I just wanted to stop and admire the artwork like so many other people had done before me. I kept praying under my breath, binding the scenes that I was being shown in the spirit, binding them in Jesus's name, and then I wondered to myself how many untimely deaths these walls had witnessed. If they could only talk, what kind of stories they could tell! Even stranger to me was how I could be in this place that was known as one of the centers of the Christian faith, and I felt like I was surrounded by a great deal of darkness. The catacombs that we had toured the day before were dark and haunting places to my friend; they were scary to him because he allowed fear to follow him most of the time. But I was led around the dark and dusty tunnels by angels of light, and the catacombs, where literally thousands of Christians had found their final resting places, I had felt at peace. I also knew that I was sensing everything in the spirit. I had realized that in seasons of my life where I wasn't being spiritually sharpened, my ability to see in the spirit was almost never turned off. In this fairly depleted state, I saw everything and could feel the sorrow of the spirits that were here in these places long before me.

My friend and I decided to go have lunch; he said he felt as if he had put me through enough for one morning. While we were eating, he asked me if I had ever been to Castel Sant'Angelo, which was a castle that had been acquired by the Vatican City in the 1700s and had harbored several popes fleeing for their lives from the Vatican during numerous uprisings. It sounded like a good way to spend the afternoon, and the next thing I knew, we were at Ponte Sant'Angelo, a bridge that took us from Rome over the river Tiber. The first things that I noticed as we started walking across the bridge were the beautiful statues of angels on either side, but as we passed the first set of angel statues, I started getting a queasy feeling in my stomach. My friend asked if everything was OK.

I said, "I think so, but this dark feeling is starting to come over me again."

He replied, "That's a little funny because were in broad daylight, and that must be what I felt when we were in the catacombs yesterday."

I walked a little farther and could almost hear quiet little screams, like the sound of someone's voice being muffled as they died. I asked him just how many people had died on this bridge, and he told me that according to history, they used this bridge for executions—possibly in the thousands, so they had stopped keeping records. He asked if I would be OK to make it to the other side of the bridge.

I answered him and said, "Let's just see how this goes." And we kept walking.

By the time we reached the center of the bridge, I wasn't just sensing what had happened here; now my vision was kicking in. I stopped and grabbed hold of the handrail on one side of the bridge; it wasn't like I was seeing demonic entities—more like just dark figures moving about in the broad daylight. I couldn't tell just how many people had met untimely deaths here; it was almost like I was having flashes of some of these executions. The screams I was hearing were rather soft, but only because in my mind I was trying to block them out. Without my even knowing it, we had reached the other side of the bridge.

Now walking on the grounds in front of Castel Sant'Angelo, I stopped and gathered my thoughts. My tour-guide friend stated, "I don't remember your girlfriend being this sensitive to the dark entities we came in contact with in Rome."

I said, "First of all, she was not my girlfriend, and second of all, she used to play games with them most of the time."

He said, "I don't think she would have enjoyed the catacombs as much as you did."

I'm not really sure if he understood the difference between her and me. All he knew was that we could both see in the supernatural realm, and even though he was a Christian, I wasn't sure that he completely understood how this gift worked.

As I looked around the grounds in the natural, it was all so fascinating, but I was pretty sure that as soon as we got closer to the castle, the things that I was looking at in the natural would start to blend into what I was seeing in the spirit. As we started to walk into the castle grounds, I asked my friend, "What is that you see or feel when you walk in to these historic places?"

He said, "I just see history that comes to life: beautiful buildings, paintings, and statues. That's why I'm curious to see what it is you see in the spirit, because it's part of the history that I can never experience. So I do my best to experience it through your eyes. Is anything manifesting to you in the spirit before we get to the castle?"

I said, "No, but I was curious about the angel on top of the dome."

He said, "Oh, that's the archangel Michael, and in truth he is the sixth one to be up there; the others were all destroyed either by nature or by battles. Have you ever seen the archangel Michael?"

"No," I answered. "So if you're wondering if the representation is accurate, I have to assume other seers could answer that question better than me."

He said, "OK, I was just checking."

Walking into the castle, I realized that I was probably entering by the same steps that ancient kings and popes had also walked. I didn't see into the spirit, but I could feel a multitude of emotions whirling around me, as if every part of me was engaged except for my eyes. I could hear sounds, voices, words that I could not understand, possibly in Italian but I wasn't sure. My friend wanted to know what I was seeing. I told him there wasn't much happening at the moment but that I was hearing a voice.

He asked, "How can you hear a single voice over the chatter of the tourists?"

I said, "I know it's strange, but it's like I'm supposed to hear one voice, and everything else fades away into the background."

He asked, "Can you make out what you're hearing, a name or phrase?"

I answered him and said, "I'm not sure yet, but when I can, you will be the first to know."

We went through some beautiful rooms with sculptures and frescoes, and still there were these voices that almost sounded like rushing water, but there were distinct words being said. As always, I prayed quietly under my breath. We then passed through to some of the rooms, and the voices I was hearing became louder and clearer.

I asked my friend, "Who or what is Bugatti?"

He smiled and said, "Why? Is that the word you're hearing?"

I said, "Something like that. Instead of sounding like rushing water, it sounds more like cries of fear."

My tour-guide friend said, "Bugatti was the name of a very famous and long-standing executioner in this castle, and I have no doubt his name brought fear to many prisoners that were kept here. I'm guessing that the voices you are hearing are getting louder because the next room we are going into is the prison, along with the torture chamber."

I said, "Oh, sure, let's take the guy that sees into the supernatural into another place where human beings were tortured and beaten." At that moment it was no longer sounds and the sensing in the spirit; it was darkness in a well-lit room. It was fear moving about, trying its best to show short little movies in people's unsuspecting minds of what horrors and events surely took place in this sinister part of the castle. The prayers that I had been praying under my breath may have gotten louder here, hopefully not drawing attention to myself, but in my own way, I was trying to keep the demonic entities from putting thoughts in my mind. There was no angelic presence in this particular part of the castle, only darkness and despair. My tour-guide friend told me there was a small courtyard where we could sit for a minute and get some air, in my mind I thought that was a good idea. But in the very second that we walked out into the air, the spiritual presence of death grew stronger.

I said to my friend, "This courtyard is somehow even spiritually darker than the prison and torture chamber. In the spirit there is far more fear here than anywhere else, and the haunting sound of the name 'Bugatti' is much stronger here. This courtyard is a place where he performed the executions, isn't it?"

He answered, "Yes. Are you OK?"

I said to him, "There is a great deal of blood in these bricks, and in many ways, I feel like the ground is crying out, but not to me. There has been so much death here by so many executioners, but the name I kept hearing over and over was *Bugatti*."

I thought to myself how many must have died at the hands of this one man. I asked my friend if he had any idea of how many people this executioner had killed. He said that Bugatti was the executioner here for over sixty-five years and that he had recorded 516 executions—but those were only the ones that had been recorded.

All I knew was I could only stay in this courtyard for a short period of time. I didn't want to allow the spirit of deception to put any thoughts into my mind, so as usual while seeing these dark entities in the spirit, I prayed quietly under my breath. The entities would appear to me as shadows cast on a wall, but there was no wall in the middle of this courtyard, and the entities were originating from the bricks themselves. Every now and then, they would take the forms of demonic spirits that I was accustomed to seeing for so long. Some would even stretch themselves as if to appear larger and then shrink back down and move away. My prayers, like always, kept them at bay, and once in a while, the entities would manifest with a hood covering their face and what looked like a large-bladed ax in their hand; some had large mallets. I didn't even know that was a thing, but my friend explained that they use those as well. The mallet-looking item was called a poleaxe, and that method of execution was called *mazzatello*. It caused severe head trauma, and at least in my opinion, it sounded a lot more painful. At this point I'm sure the entities knew they couldn't inflict any pain with their manifested weapons, but no doubt they had hoped that they would invoke the sense of fear. I have to wonder if they were doing this because they knew that I could see into the spirit, because in the natural, the courtyard was peaceful with the statue of an angel looking on as if to say to the tourists that this was a heavenly place of peace.

I suppose everything in life and death is about perspective, but in this case, I was pretty sure that my perspective was far different from the other people taking photographs by the statue and at the steps. In their eyes it was all history, but for those who are able to see into the spiritual realm, it was very dark and real. Going up the steps as we left the courtyard, I stopped to look back, and people were still snapping pictures, talking and laughing. The spirits that I had seen while standing on these bricks faded away and all I could see from the steps were people. My tour guide said we would head back toward the bridge, but as we walked slowly back through the castle, it felt like the rooms and the hallways as we traveled were all being revealed to me in the same fashion as the courtyard had been. It was as if all the manifestations that I had seen in this castle began to converge on me at once, so I stopped and prayed a soft prayer binding these entities around me in Jesus's name and casting them out. At once everything became still and quiet. I'm not sure if anyone else noticed the sudden sense of calmness that was surrounding us, but I did.

This climate of peace stayed with us as we walked out into the open air toward the front of the castle. It was so tranquil, like taking a deep breath of fresh air. My friend and I talked back and forth as we walked toward the bridge; many people were coming and going. As we stepped out onto the bridge, continuing our way back to where our car had been parked, I was feeling pretty good about how things around me had diminished and was not really paying attention to where I was going. I suddenly stopped, feeling as if I were going to walk into the back of the man in front of me. My friend kept walking, not noticing my abrupt stop. As I went to sidestep around the man, he turned to look at me. Everything inside me was saying, *This is an evil spirit. Do not give it place.* So as it was opening its mouth to speak, I bound it in Jesus's name. As I kept walking, the crowds of people that I thought were coming and going turned out to be more entities than people, and the closer I moved into the center of the bridge, once again the bloodstains on the bricks became more pronounced. Even though other people were talking, I could still hear the whispers of the bloodshed crying out, softly, quietly. It was as if my ears were more in tune to what was being said in the spiritual as opposed to the chatter that was going on in the natural. It was only because of my own curiosity, and in some ways my lack of faith, that I even allowed these entities, these voices, to continue. And then, as if remembering I had been given dominion over them, I cast them out and away from me.

It was then that I heard my friend's voice saying, "Why do you walk so slowly?" He stood on the pavement on the other side.

I smiled and said, "If this bridge wasn't so crowded, I could have kept up with you."

He began to laugh, and I looked around to see no one on the bridge but us.

He said, "Crowded in your eyes."

But for me, I was just ready to go eat dinner. When we returned to his car, he asked me what it was I saw on the bridge, I told him that at first it looked like a great deal of tourists, but as I looked closer, none of them had recognizable faces, and I couldn't tell in the spirit what it was they were saying, but I knew there had been many atrocities committed on that bridge. He asked me about the angels' statues on the bridge, and I told him that I believed that was man's way of covering up the sins that had been committed; we tend to look at things like statues of angels and saints, popes, and martyrs and think to ourselves this must be a godly place, a holy place. But in truth I believe its man's way of covering up our mistakes, like trying to whitewash a fence to cover up the stains of our past. Our past is our past, and at the very best, we can ask for forgiveness, to try to learn from our mistakes and not repeat them. Repentance is a powerful tool, and if used truthfully, it can redirect the course of a mighty ship. But no amount of whitewash can cover the stains committed by any man. Only the blood of Jesus can truly set us free, and only by walking in his path and seeking his word can the stains of our lives truly be covered.

Chapter 2: Shiny Pennies

Returning back to the base from my time in Italy, I was asked if I thought I was up to going on some training missions. Of course, I jumped at the chance, and on one of these training jumps, we were flying in an AC-130—just a normal day at the office—but this time, instead of being with my well-seasoned team, I was with a bunch of newbies. Being able to see in the spirit showed me many things, and one thing I knew without question was exactly what fear looked like. There was a small group of guys who were going to jump, but two of the guys whom I was to jump with were more nervous than the rest. I didn't ask them many questions; I just knew what I needed to do. I knelt between them and said, "When that bay door opens, what you need to do is stare out at the horizon. Find something to fix your eyes on, and don't look away. And when you're told to, calmly pull your primary chute, and as best you can, just breathe normal. Remember, no fear. We have been trained to do this; you know what to do. No fear."

With that, I put one hand on each of their shoulders and said a quick prayer. After I said "Amen," I repeated again, "No fear! Remember, I will be close, but God will be closer; he will never leave you, nor forsake you."

With that the bay door opened, and one of the non-commissioned officers (NCO) said, "OK, boys, it's time to do what you were trained to do. I'll see you back at the base after they pick you up."

I stood up, and we walked back toward the bay door in the rear of the plane. I looked at my trainees and said, "I'll see you two on the ground."

As we jumped off the deck one by one, I made sure to keep my two guys in sight, and as our signal went off and the chutes deployed, I felt a sense of relief. Every time you jump, you put your faith in God's hands, in your gear, and in the blessed hands of the ground crew who packs your gear.

Once we got to the ground and were gathering up our chutes, we were to move to a designated area and wait to be extracted. I noticed the two guys whom I had talked to up in the plane were having a loud conversation. I asked them, "Was that awesome or what?"

One of them said, "The jump was great, but explain to us why we both saw you shining like a brand-new penny as we were dropping from that plane."

I said, "Maybe you guys caught me in the suns light just right, or maybe God's presence is on me. I'll let you pick."

It just so happens that our extraction point was near a small lake, and these guys didn't know it because we were carrying MREs (meals ready to eat), but if I had my way, we were going to have fish for dinner. I was well known for bringing fishing line, hooks, and sometimes other fishing equipment. When I was a kid growing up, my dad taught me how to clean and cook fish on an open fire, so after things got settled; I went and caught us some dinner. Afterward, one of the new guys told me he really didn't like fish, but he was afraid to tell me that after I went and caught and prepared it for them.

The next day our ride showed up in a clearing nearby. We were ready and were able to get to our transportation quickly; our ride came by way of several Huey helicopters. Before long we were back on base, and my new airmen were already telling war stories. As we were walking back to our unit, one of the two guys whom I had prayed for while we were in the air ran up next to me and said, "When we were up in that 130, how did you know what I was feeling?"

I said, "God has given me a way of just knowing these things, and you must remember that wasn't my first time up; I know what it looks like."

The young man said, "I think it was more the God thing, because after you prayed for me, I really didn't feel scared anymore. I felt like God had sent an angel to escort me to the ground and give me the confidence that I needed."

I asked him, "Are you a Christian?"

He said, "My parents are more than I am. I accepted Jesus in my life when I was a kid, but I really don't go to church anymore."

He and I talked for quite a while, and he said that he was going to tell his mom about me so that she would know that her prayers were being answered.

As I arrived back at the air station and my dorm once again, there was mail waiting for me. It was a letter from my dad saying that he was really looking forward to starting this business with me if I had made the decision to get out of the military. Starting my own business looked like a possible answer for what I was to do in my future, and my current leadership had told me in so many words that I would be returning to the maintenance shop. They had felt that after my time in the burn unit, I was not capable of doing my job that I was cross-trained into. So that week I made a decision to start my paperwork for separation from the military. Looking back, it was one of those life-changing decisions that at some point you regret and at other times you praise God that you chose the path you did. I'm not sure why I wanted to give my dad so many opportunities when he had failed me so many times; maybe it was because God had given me endless opportunities when I had failed so many times. So now with my date of separation (DOS) in place, I prepared myself for this transition. There were many appointments to attend, and there was even more paperwork to fill out. I also had the cars, bought while in country (my old reliable Mercedes-Benz and Porsche 911), that needed to be sold off before I left. I also had to make phone calls to my dad to look for certification schools, as well as a possible location for the business venture we were planning.

If the Ruins Could Speak

I decided to visit some of the neighboring ruins in the area where I lived because I didn't know if or when I would ever come back to Germany. I had seen these castle ruins for years now and had never set foot in them, so I decided that before I left what had been my home for the last three and a half years, I was going to go by myself and see what was there. There was one particular castle that I could see from the dorm parking lot up on the hill. I was still in pretty good shape, so I found a walking path to this forgotten ruin. It was known in the area as the Hohenecken Castle, and it was built sometime around the 1200s; the castle overlooked the city of Kaiserslautern. The castle's destruction began in 1525 during the Persian War, when the Persians laid siege to the castle, destroying a large part of it. In a later war with the French in 1689, the castle was again blown up by enemy cannon balls. Walking among the ruins, I was unable to see anything in the spirit, but from time to time, placing my hands upon the ruined walls, I was able to sense a multitude of feelings, both dark spirits and those of ministering spirits. Without question many people had lived and died here, but that could be said about any place in the world that had seen as much war as this country had. Another nearby castle that I had often seen due to its proximity to the hospital that I often visited in Landstuhl, Germany, was the Nanstine Castle that was built around 1162 by Emperor Frederick. The castle had survived many sieges throughout the years, but reconstruction had taken place in 1542 and 1595 as well. Walking through the outside of the castle in the sunshine was very beautiful; in the spirit it was the same—bright and incredible to see. But once the sun started to set, things began to change; things that in the daylight seemed majestic now began to feel ominous. Visitors to the castle even started to talk about the ghosts that would haunt this ruin once the sun began to set; it was like they expected a manifestation. Some of the visitors allowed a spirit of fear to overtake them, and they hurried to leave with their families, frightened that they, too, would witness the hauntings of what they said were undead spirits. Within about thirty minutes, all of the visitors had left the ruins except for me and one other couple who had come together to experience some type of supernatural entity. The woman looked amazed that I was there by myself. She asked me if I was here to see if there were actually ghosts in the castle. I told her that in my opinion, if people want the manifestation of a dark spirit, that's probably what is going to happen. I asked her if she wanted to see ghosts, and she said, "No, not really."

The guy who was with her appeared to be a little bothered that she was talking to me, so he grabbed her by the hand and walked off in a different direction. I was OK with this because I was by myself anyway, and I didn't expect anyone to stay with me after dark except for the people who were the overseers, and they, too, were surprised that I would walk around the ruins alone. The castle was illuminated from the outside only, so any light that would shine in would shine in through windows or in places where the walls had begun to crumble. In the daylight many of these areas in the castle were photo opportunities, but in the darkness, they became shadows where only entities of fear would manifest.

It wasn't more than fifteen minutes that I heard a woman's scream, immediately followed by the startled sounds of her male escort. I was in the courtyard looking out over a wall when I heard the sounds, and I couldn't tell where the woman ran out from, but looking down, I saw her friend had become so frightened that he face-planted into a wall and was trying to regather himself so that he could stand up and continue his sprint out of the building. Seeing in the spirit allowed me to observe several dark entities that intertwined with the shadows of the castle. They had taken the form of what looked like smoke moving about in the areas that weren't well lit. After the screams had faded, the demons must have felt that fear was going to overtake me as well, and they started manifesting before me. At first, they took on a smoke type of manifestation, and when that didn't create fear in me as they had hoped, they decided that taking on the form of disfigured people, almost like zombies, should do the trick. With this manifestation, I decided to whisper under my breath, "I bind you evil spirits in Jesus's name and cast you out of my presence."

And with that, the manifestation of deception and fear left. Other than the caretakers of the castle, I was in these ruins by myself and wanted to see if any other entities would appear to me. I continued to walk around the inside of the castle, weaving my way in and out of the shadows. I came to an archway that looked like a tunnel, and at the end where the light from the outside was shining in, I could see the outline of a person. At first, I thought it was one of the caretakers of the castle who was checking to see if any visitors were still on the premises. I called to the caretaker and asked if it was time for me to leave. I could only make out the silhouette of the person. They turned and started to walk, but it was hard to tell if they were walking to me or away from me.

I said again, "I'm sorry if I'm holding you up; do I need to leave?"

The voice that came back to me was not that of the caretaker. The voice said in a low tone, "You should've left when the others ran away in fear."

Because we were in a tunnel, it sounded like the person was right in front of me, but they were actually quite a distance away. So, being foolish, I decided to walk toward this silhouette. If it was walking toward me, we would meet in the middle, but if it was walking away, I had planned on following it. It turned out it was the latter, and I felt like this entity wanted me to follow them—so who was I not to be compliant? I had lost sight of the silhouette as I was walking through this arched tunnel, and when I reached the compartment on the other side, I could no longer see the silhouette; there didn't appear to be any other way other than back through the arched tunnel. I turned and continued back the way I had come. Once I reached the other end, I called out and said, "Are you still here, or are you in fear?"

No reply came back to me. But as I returned back to what looked like a courtyard, the lights from the outside of the structure once again allowed some of the areas to be dimly lit and others to be pitch black. In this type of light, my eyes were trying to adjust, and I could see the same silhouette in a dark, shadowy area off to one side of the courtyard. I walked straight to it, but this time the figure stayed put and didn't move away. I asked the entity why it had manifested to me in this way, and the entity informed me that it had always manifested in this way. I asked, "What do you mean by 'always'?"

And the entity replied, "For hundreds of years, I've taken on this form. Why has fear not overtaken you?"

I replied, "I have authority in the name of the Lord Jesus Christ and in the word. It says that I shall not allow fear to overtake me."

The dark spirit replied and said, "Then I will leave you so that you will not use your authority to cast me out." And in the next moment, the entity was gone.

As I was leaving the castle, the caretakers addressed me in German, and when I paused, they asked me the same question in English and said, "Did you see any ghosts?"

I said, "Yes, I did but the castle is clean now—at least until tomorrow night, when they return to invoke fear on a different set of tourists."

The caretakers laughed and said, "Well, at least you didn't run out of the castle yelling."

I said, "Nope, not today."

Chapter 3: Manifestations in Flight

Early in 1987 I was to board a plane from the Rhein-Main airbase in Germany to a base on the East Coast to be officially discharged from active duty military. I was booked on a civilian flight, but we were to be dressed in our military uniforms (dress blues) until we reached our destination on the other side of the big pond. It was a large aircraft with mostly civilian passengers, but there were a few other military members as well. I always felt strange being in an aircraft and having no access to a parachute, a little like walking around a shopping mall with no pants on. Soon after takeoff, I introduced myself to an army soldier who was seated next to me. He was also being discharged once we reached our final destination. He said he really didn't like riding on airplanes that much and tried to do it as little as possible; he told me that once we reached the ground on the East Coast, he didn't care if he had to ride ten hours on a bus—he wasn't going to fly again. We were seated near the back of the plane, and I was on the aisle, so I could see all the way to the front of the plane without too many heads in my way. About an hour into the flight, as my new friend and I were still talking, I noticed two demonic entities that had appeared with what looked like two men sitting on either side of the aisle. The man on the right of the aisle had a demonic entity down near his feet looking back and forth up and down the aisle of the plane. The other demonic entity was only looking toward the back of the plane; it felt like he was staring right at me, but I really wasn't sure. I started wrestling with myself as to what action I should take with these demons. My army friend kept talking, but his words were being drowned out by the thoughts going through my mind as far as what I should do. Sometime during that process, I noticed an angel who was kneeling down next to me in the aisle. He said, "Seer, I am the messenger. You need to go lay hands on those two passengers that the demons have appeared with, and at that time you will cast them out. In faith you need to do this, and trust God. If you don't, it is likely that this plane will not make it to its final destination."

Under my breath I said, "Is that all? Just walk up to them, lay hands on them, and start praying?"

I was thinking to myself, *OK, that won't alarm anybody on the plane, and I'm sure the two passengers won't notice me at all!* But in my spirit, I was reminded of Peter walking off the boat, just in faith, and when he started to sink, Jesus held out his hand and walked him back to the ship safely (Matthew 14:25–32). I looked at the young man seated next to me and said, "I'll be back in a few minutes."

I stood up and started slowly walking toward the front of the plane. As I was walking, a third demonic entity appeared with the man on the right. The strange thing was that they didn't really even notice me walking toward them. Still walking, I came to the two men and just walked right past them, once again thinking to myself, *Well, that was an epic fail*. So, trying to be cool, I walked all the way to the front of the plane to where the flight attendants were. Once I arrived I struggled to think of something to say without once again looking stupid, so I asked, "About what time will the plane land on the East Coast?"

The flight attendants looked at each other and said, "Well, sir, it will be a while."

I told them, "Thank you," and turned around to start my journey back down the aisle.

As I looked up, I noticed that the third demon, which was now on the left side of the aisle, had his eyes on me. Once again, I was walking very slowly, trying to figure out exactly how I was going to do this. Right as I came up next to them, the plane hit an air pocket. It happened so fast that I was unable to prepare myself for it, and I went down on one knee. Reaching up to catch myself, one of my hands landed on the shoulder of the man on my right and the forearm of the man on my left. Quickly, I spoke under my breath and said, "In Jesus's name I bind these demonic spirits from carrying out whatever task they have been assigned on this airplane. In Jesus's name you are bound, and I cast you out in the mighty name of the Jesus."

As I looked up at the man on my left, I saw that he had short dark hair and a long beard, and on my right the man also had dark hair, but it was much longer, and he was younger than the other guy. As I was walking down the aisle toward them, I was sure they were both wide awake, but now as I looked from my knee, they looked to be sound asleep. The other thing I noticed while I was on my knee was that there was a bag under the seat of the man with the beard that was on my left.

I stood up, and some of the people near me asked, "Sir, are you all right?"

I answered, "I'm fine, thank you," and walked back down the aisle to my seat. As I sat down, the guy in the seat next to me said, "Wow, when we hit that air pocket, I saw you go down in the aisle. Are you OK?"

I said, "I'm fine."

He said, "Well, I hope you got that stewardess's phone number to make that trip all the way the front worth it."

I said, "Oh, I think the trip up front was worth it." As I sat there and tried to calm my thoughts, the flight attendant walked up and asked me if I was OK.

I said, “Yes, I’m OK, but I need to talk to you back up front if it is possible?”

She said, “Yes that’s fine.”

As I stood up, the guy next to me winked his eye and said, “Go get her, big boy!”

I smiled and followed the flight attendant back to the front of the plane. As I passed the two guys whom I had prayed over, they looked as if to be in a deep sleep. When we reached the front of the plane, she asked me again if everything was OK.

I said, “I am fine, but when I went down on one knee in the aisle, I noticed a black bag under one of the men’s seats, and I know this sounds strange, but is there any way, while they’re asleep, you could search the bag to know what the contents are?”

She said, “I will have to OK it with the pilot, but if there is anything suspicious, we have the right to check any bag on board the flight.”

She asked me to stay there, and she went to talk to one of the pilots. When she came back, there was a copilot with her. He asked me why I suspected anything.

I said, “When we hit the air pocket and I went down to my knee, I thought I saw something poking out of the bag. It may be nothing, but I would feel a lot better if someone would take a look in that bag.”

He instructed one of the flight attendants to push a trash cart down the aisle to collect any trash, and when they arrived where the two men were, to put the bag in one of the drawers and bring it back to the front. They had me sit down in one of the flight attendant's seats and wait until they returned. About ten minutes later, the flight attendant returned with the cart and the bag. They closed the curtain and carefully removed the black bag. One of the other pilots came in and inspected the bag as well. It was determined that they were going to put the bag in a safe on the plane and said that when the plane lands in the United States, someone else would inspect the contents of the bag. Then they asked me to go back to my seat and said that they would contact me later. Again, walking back to my seat, I saw the two men were still in deep sleep.

I arrived at my seat, and the guy who had been seated next to me said, "You must've hit it off pretty good with that stewardess to spend so much time up there."

I just smiled, put my seat back, and closed my eyes. When the captain announced that we would be arriving soon on the East Coast, a flight attendant came back and knelt down next to me and told me to just stay in my seat until everyone else was off the plane. I told her I would, and after we landed and everyone else was departing the aircraft, I just stayed behind, just me and my backpack.

Then the flight attendant came back and asked me to follow her, and as we walked down the aisle, I wasn't sure if the two men were asleep or maybe dead? The stewardess and another man escorted me up the ramp and to a room. I just sat there waiting for somebody to come and talk to me. Finally some men came in and sat down.

The first one said, "Well, it's a good thing God put a military man on board the flight that was paying attention. We thank you for alerting the crew of the bag that was under one of the passenger seats."

They never told me if it was a bomb or not, and I never saw the two men come off the plane. I have to assume something must've happened because they thanked me and asked me not to mention anything about the incident. Then they sent me on my way.

After I retrieved my luggage, there was a van out front of the airport to take us to the base for our discharge. The driver asked me, "So how was your flight?"

I smiled and said, "It was fine. How was your drive over here?"

He said, "Probably a lot like your flight—uneventful."

Home Sweet Home

Arriving at the military base, we were ushered in to many different rooms as well as briefings. It all happened fast, and the next thing I knew, I was standing out front in civilian clothes with a backpack, a rolling suitcase, and a duffel bag. Most of my personal items had been sent weeks earlier to my dad's address in the Midwest. Once again, I was taking a taxi to the bus station and hopping on a bus that was taking me to the town where my dad and stepmother lived. I thought about all of the bus rides I had been on while based in Germany, all the many things I had seen, both in the natural and in the spiritual. As always, I had high expectations for where I was going and what I was about to get into with my dad, as well as hopefully finding a church that was like the one I'd attended back home in California. By this time in my spiritual walk, I felt depleted. For the year or so that I attended church when I was first saved, I had been spiritually built up, but now after being in the military for nearly six years, as far as my teaching, I was in a low point and needed guidance as to how I was to move forward in my Christian walk. My dad or stepmother couldn't help me in this area; they were under the impression that you really didn't need to go to a church to know God. What I knew was that my spiritual gas gauge was down near empty, and for me, when that was the case; I went back to seeing in the spirit every hour of the day. It was exhausting, and I needed to have my spiritual fuel tank refilled. I knew that I was going to face the same old demonic entities that I had faced as a kid when I went to my dad and stepmom's house, and in the spiritual it was something like going into battle without being properly fed. I would be OK for a short period of time, and after that I would become exhausted in the battle.

Arriving at the bus station in the Midwest was fairly scary because I had what you might call a déjà vu moment; it was all too familiar. My dad was standing there waiting for me, and after collecting my luggage, we walked to his truck put my stuff in the back and started the short trip to his house. I asked him if he was able to find any buildings that might be suitable for the business that we wanted to start, but he said no, that he hadn't really looked at all.

While I was still overseas, I had found a school that we could go to and learn about key making, safes, and alarm systems. I hadn't paid for anything yet because I didn't know if both of us would be going or just me. My dad had received many opportunities over the years to start businesses but for some reason always lacked the confidence to move forward and take the risk. I, on the other hand, just wanted to give God a chance to improve my life both spiritually and financially.

When we got to the house and my dad opened the garage door, I noticed that all of the boxes that I had sent from Germany were piled up in his garage.

I looked at my dad and said, "No room in the house?"

He said, "Sorry. Your stepmom thought it would be better to leave them out here."

I thought to myself, *The more things change, the more things stay the same*. As we went in the house from the garage, we started up the stairs to the landing by the front door, turning to go up to the second level of the house. On the railing by the stairs, I noticed once again three demonic entities just looking at me as if they were dogs waiting for an unwanted guest. My stepmom was seated at the table in the kitchen. She had put on a good deal of weight since the last time I had seen her, and as always she had a large pill container sitting in front of her, and her hands were shaking. As I approached her, one of the demons climbed up the back of her chair and began speaking to her. I said hello and asked her how she was feeling.

She said, "I would get up, but I am feeling terrible and think it best that I stay seated."

The demonic entity looked at me with a crooked grin. I walked over to the kitchen window and looked out into the woods behind my dad and stepmom's house, and under my breath I said, "In

Jesus's name, demonic entities, you have no place in this house, and I cast you out in Jesus's name."

As I turned around, two of the demonic entities quickly left the room, but the one that had climbed up the back of my stepmother's chair walked off slowly and looked over his shoulder at me, as if to be a bit defiant.

The upstairs bathroom was near my stepmother's room, so I followed the demon to see where it was going. I excused myself, saying that I had to go use the bathroom. As it slowly walked, I thought it went into my stepmother's room and just crouched in the corner to the right of her bed. I turned back around and went into the restroom. When I came out and went back into the kitchen, I asked my stepmother if she was feeling any better. She said, "I'm feeling good enough to possibly eat something and play a game of dice."

They allowed me to stay downstairs in the basement until I was able to get a place of my own. In the daytime when my dad was at work, I would go to my classes at a local trade school college. At the gym where I had started working out, the owner said that he would allow me to work out there for free if I would stay on from time to time as a personal trainer, so that's what I did. I had also gotten a job as a bouncer at a large well-known hotel that had a nightclub on the first floor. My days were pretty busy by design so that I would not spend much time at their house, only to sleep. The problem was I didn't really make enough money to get a place of my own, and I knew that every day I was at their house I was one day closer to wearing out my welcome. My dad told me that the manufacturing company where he worked had a full-time opening and they would probably hire me right away. The only glitch was that it was from midnight to 8:00 a.m., but it did pay well, and I would be able to afford to get an apartment on my own.

The one thing about keeping myself overly busy was if I was seeing in the spirit, it was only for a short time, and if I didn't pay attention to them, they just became like someone else in the room. I think that my challenge with church is that I was trying to find one like the church I was saved in when I was younger. In that church I would see angelic movement and things happening in the spirit. It was so common that it became routine, but I loved it. In the churches that I would visit here, there was no spiritual movement at all, like a spiritually sterile environment, the same as I felt when I was in the military and would go to the base chapel. The people were always very nice and welcoming, but at the same time, I felt like if I were to say anything about seeing in the spirit or the lack thereof, they would probably be offended. Even though I was around good and well-meaning

Christian brothers and sisters, for now I would have to stay spiritually silent.

Moving to the City

The locksmith classes that I was taking were coming to an end, and I had collected some of the equipment that we would need to open our own shop, but as I had earlier anticipated, the closer we came to going out and actually opening a business, the colder my dad's feet became. He said that he couldn't give up his Monday through Friday job, and I understood that, but he said he wouldn't be able to help me when he got off work or on weekends because my stepmom needed him to help her. I was living in my own place by this time and wasn't sure if I could keep up my work pace full time. I had met some guys at the nightclub, where I was still working part time, and they worked for a construction company that was hired to build a large chain of hotels. They said that they were getting ready to go up to a large Midwest City and build a new hotel. If I wanted to join them, they would hire me and pay me a lot more than I was making. The timing was good for me because my half-brother had been recently separated from his wife and was living by himself near the same city where the new hotel would be constructed. We had always gotten along great, and he said that he would welcome a roommate to help him with the bills as well as the company.

I had used a lot of the money I had saved from the military buying equipment and schooling for the lock-and-security business, but my brother said that until the job started, I wouldn't have to pay much. With that, I moved in with my brother, and shortly thereafter I started work on the construction site building an eight-story hotel near the international airport.

My brother and I were a lot alike in the fact that we were both Christians that were in search of a church that we both felt at home in. At this point in time, I didn't really feel like my brother needed to know that I was able to see in the spirit, but I was in faith that I would find a church that could at least understand what it was that I was able to do. I'm not really sure why it was such a mystery to people who read the Bible because when I was first saved; my pastor had shown me many passages that discussed my particular gifting. It was like everyone wanted to talk about the other gifts of the spirit but ignore mine, so once again I had to say to myself, "Hello, silence, my old friend."

At one point we went to a larger church, and to my surprise, there were multiple angels positioned outside of the church. When I discreetly walked over near them, one of the angels said something to the angel standing next to him, and as we walked in, one of them from a distance followed as we walked through the door. We introduced ourselves to some of the people, but I kept my eye on this one angel. It was not as large as some of the angels I'd seen at my old church, but it was quite a bit taller than I. Then we went into a large sanctuary, and there was another angel that was on the platform to one side of the stage. We sat down, and soon the praise and worship began. It didn't feel like home, but it was the closest thing that I had experienced to home in a long time. The message was wonderful, and this would be the church that we would go to for quite some time. I never got to know the pastors or staff, and in truth I never really allowed myself to get involved in any of the ministries in this church. I think it was due to lack of my own effort that I was never comfortable enough to tell them that there were angels in their midst.

By this time, we had moved from the friend's house that we were living in to a very nice duplex. Everything in my life at this point was going well. We lived in a nice place; I had a good job (although I knew it was temporary because when the hotel was finished, I would be out of a job). They would all move on to the next construction site, and I would have a choice to make: whether to follow them or stay here with my brother. My weight lifting was going great; we had a nice selection of weights in our garage, and I was also training in public gyms from time to time. I enjoyed working in construction due to the physical nature of the work. I felt like I would work out throughout the day and get paid for it and then go home and train more specific muscle groups. Everything they would have me do in construction my mind would warp into something that had to do with weight lifting, so I really did enjoy every minute of it. At about the midpoint of the construction project, they asked me if I would be able to move on with them to the next job. At that time I wasn't sure what I wanted to do, so I told them I was still thinking about it. The fact was I really did like living with my brother, but I also enjoyed doing the construction work as well. Leaning more toward staying here, I started looking for other options for work. Beings I was a veteran and had some medical training both before I came in the military as well as while I was in the military, I decided to put in an application at a local medical center. As I continued to work in construction on the hotel, I didn't realize how many different interviews I would have to go through to get a job at the medical center. As the completion of the hotel neared, I finally received the word that I would be starting at the medical center the following week. God's timing is perfect.

Chapter 4: Sensing the Outcome

I had never worked in an actual hospital; I had worked in the medical field off and on for quite some time, but this was the first time working in the actual facility, and it was a continuous learning experience. They started me out working in the medical intensive care unit (MICU). It was stressful at times getting used to this new job, but both in the natural and in supernatural realms, it was fascinating. I came to the realization that maybe God had brought me here for an actual purpose. I wasn't able to tell people that I could see demonic entities or angels with them, but one thing became very apparent: both entities were playing a crucial role in the outcomes of these patients.

To this point, I had never been instructed much about the process of a spiritual healing. I knew that healing was in the Bible, but either I had never really been taught about it, or maybe it was that I didn't listen because I didn't need it. Either way people who were in this unit, at least when they first arrived, were in a delicate spiritual balancing act. Some, from the moment they came in, had an angel with them, and still others had a demonic presence that kept them from ever crossing that bridge back into a healthy situation. As bad as it sounds, I could almost tell you with great accuracy who would be walking out of the hospital and who would be taking a trip to the basement and the morgue. My job was to help in the process of healing and move them on to a general hospital room for the remainder of the recovery. The hard part for me was their loved ones coming to visit; they would ask me how the patient was doing, and depending on what spiritual presence was in that room, I would either be very sure about the recovery, or I would be very neutral and not lean one way or the other. On the upside, when I was spiritually sure that the patient's recovery looked good and their loved ones would come in expecting the worst, I was able to tell them, "You have to have faith; your loved one will experience a full recovery." But on the other hand, I wasn't really sure what to tell people that I didn't feel so confident in, so I would tend to speak very generally and in medical terminology. At times I would have short conversations with some of the angelic beings, and there were times that the angels were there to take the patient home—not an earthly home but an angelic one.

For the patients who came in with a demonic presence, I would try to get to them as soon as I could to bind and cast out the demonic entity as soon as possible. Often, when I would come back the next day for my shift, the entity would reappear to me. Again, I would repeat the process, and in these cases, the patient's recovery would go up and down. Sometimes the charge nurse would say to me that things appeared to go smoother when I was on shift, but I knew it had very little to do with me and much more to do with the presence of God.

I don't know how all hospitals work, but at this medical center, they would only leave you in one section of the hospital for about three months and then move you to another section. I liked the MICU and felt like it was a good fit for me, but within a few months, I was told that I would be going to the pulmonary intensive care unit (PICU). It turned out it was a lot like the MICU, but the patients who came in had altogether different medical problems; however, in the spiritual realm, it looked the same. In the PICU it appeared as though a lot of the people came in with demonic entities. In some cases, I believe through the power of prayer as well as me casting out demons on a daily basis, many of the patients who I thought were destined to go to the morgue ended up being moved to a regular hospital room and from there discharged. As much as I knew that prayer was an important part of being a Christian, what I didn't realize was how powerful it could be. When some of the loved ones would come in to visit the patients, it was evident very quickly as to the ones who were trusting God for healing and the ones who had just flat-out given up on a recovery.

One time I noticed an angel standing at the foot of the patient's bed. The patient was on a respirator and still unconscious. Some of the patients loved ones were praying for them, and a woman had her hand on the patient's left foot. As I watched from the doorway, I noticed the angel had moved up the right side of the patient and placed his left hand on the patient's chest. Within minutes the patient opened their eyes and began to talk. At that point I went and got the charge nurse. She notified the doctor, and they took the patient off the breathing machine and replaced it with oxygen only. You don't have to tell me that prayer works. Being that I was not a registered nurse (RN), some of the staff would treat me like I was part of the janitorial service, but still others would echo what I had heard before: that it was as if the shift would run smoother when I was there. Before long I was moved from the PICU to a medical surgery unit. Not only was I able to help patients both pre- and post-operation, but from time to time, they would even allow me to go in and observe or aid in the actual surgical room operations. This was fascinating to me, firstly because we were trained in the military to do some surgical procedures in the field when necessary, but never in an environment like this. The other interesting part on the supernatural side was that I was able to watch in the spirit as angelic beings would move doctors', nurses', and anesthesiologists' hands from time to time. The angel would stand behind someone on the surgical floor and would move their hand by sliding the angelic hand into that person like the angel was wearing a glove. It was fascinating to watch. Most of the people that I came in contact with both in preoperation and post operation would have either very little spiritual activity, or I would very often see angels with them. On this floor I would see very few demonic entities with the patients, but as was the case when dealing with people, I could always sense a slight presence. At times I would go into some of the patients' rooms to do vitals or answer a call button, and I would see three or four angels in the room. They didn't really talk to me, but they would acknowledge me. I have to assume that maybe one of the angels belonged to the person who was actually in the bed, and the others were there due to the prayers of loved ones. I enjoyed working in this unit because there was a lot of peace on this floor, and death in most cases wasn't knocking on the door, as well as the demonic entities being at a minimum. But as always in the hospital, this, too, would end, and I would be moved on to a different unit.

My next stop would be in the emergency room (ER). They would do their best to bring me into this as slowly as possible to try to get me acclimated to the fast pace, but the only thing that had prepared me for this type of environment was my military training. Minus the hostile environment, it was at times on the same level. It felt like you were dropped into the middle of a landslide, and it was either keep up or get out of the way. When your shift was over, you would just have to go someplace to sit down and try to slow your own heartbeat back down to normal.

It wasn't always like that, but more often than not, it did move very quickly. It was during the weekdays that it was slower, but the closer you got to the weekend, it would start ramping up. It was here that I would first notice in the spirit that on occasion, angels as well as demonic entities were sometimes no farther away than a curtain hanging on a rod apart. There were times that they would bring in critically injured patients, and as we would frantically move about the room, I would notice an angelic being. Glancing up at the angel from time to time during my tasks, sometimes the angel would hold out its hand; it looked like to me they were escorting the individual out of the room. Shortly after that the patient would flat line, and we would bring out the paddles and try to revive them. Sometimes we were able to bring them back; sometimes I suppose they didn't want to come back. One of the patterns that I began to notice was that many of the patients who would come in to the ER with different types of sicknesses often had demonic entities with them. Almost all of the repeat visitors into the ER were accompanied by a demonic spirit of fear. What I had learned over the years was that the spirit of deception, if allowed, would manifest into demonic spirits, one of which was the entity of fear. Many of these people that would come into the ER every week were being deceived by this same spirit of fear. In the medical world, they call this hypochondria, but in the supernatural realm, it just looked like the spirit of fear. These unfortunate people would speak themselves into a multitude of symptoms, and by way of their own thoughts and words would convince themselves that they were indeed sick, and the doctors who refused to agree with them had no idea in the world how to diagnose them as patients.

At the time when I was assigned to the emergency room, there was a well-known epidemic sweeping across the country known as the AIDS virus. At the time we were required to test almost everyone, and regardless of what people came into the ER for, they were often relieved to know that they came back with a negative result. This spirit of deception that was allowed to graduate into a spirit of fear made many people worry that they were subjected to this disease, and the truth was that most of the same people had no idea of the facts or how it was contracted in the first place. But week in and week out, they would come into the emergency room to be tested or felt like they had symptoms that they were sure was due to this virus. Many rumors were spreading, and the demonic entity of deception was allowing the news channels as well as word of mouth from everyday people to confuse the average citizen as to what was the truth and what was an exaggeration. Once the exaggeration was accepted, then the demonic entity of fear would take over and was allowed to move throughout the land like a wildfire. Rumors and lack of knowledge are hard to control. It is only by educating yourself and not allowing the spirit of deception to take root in your thoughts and mind that you can quench the fiery darts of the evil one. For it is in Jesus's name that we bind these thoughts that come to us before they have a chance to manifest in reality.

We would often have homeless individuals who would come to us for a number of reasons. My heart would always go out to these unfortunate souls who somehow had lost their way along life's path, and if it was calm enough on the shift, I would try to take time to sit in the room with them to pray and just talk.

One of the men once told me, "When I was a high school senior, I never would have imagined that I would be a homeless man later on in life, but here I am."

I guess the reason that I felt as I did for these people was because at one time in my young life, I was homeless as well, and had I taken a different path, I may have been in the same situation that these people were in. Whenever possible, I would stay after my shift just to let them talk. I was someone willing to listen, having an idea of what it was like to be wearing their shoes—or the lack thereof.

In the ER most would recover and either is sent on to a hospital room or discharged, but occasionally we would lose the patient. Being that I was the low man on the totem pole, they would put the deceased person on a gurney and cover them with a sheet, and I would have to take them down to the morgue in the basement. Every time I went down to the morgue, I would see at least one or two demonic entities; only on occasion would I see any angelic being. Sometimes the family members would be down there to view or identify their deceased loved ones, and there would be angels surrounding them. I didn't really like being down there, so I usually made the trip back up to the ER quickly. On one trip down to the morgue, they had me take a new person with me so I could show them the process. Being that the ER was on the first floor and the morgue was only one floor below us, it was a short trip on an elevator, but for some of the new people, being in an elevator with a dead person was creepy; for me it was just an unfortunate part of the job. On this one occasion with a new person helping me, we got into the elevator, and as it sometimes happens, the dead body started having a bad case of the twitches. I'm not sure that I had ever seen a demonic entity of fear overtake someone quite that fast. I really thought that this person was going to try to crawl up the stainless-steel walls of the elevator and possibly attempt to crawl out the escape hatch in the top of the elevator to get out, but instead they just crumpled up into a ball in the corner of the elevator. Trying not to laugh, I told this demonic entity of fear that in Jesus's name, it would have to leave, and when we got back to the ER, my new person swore they would never take a body down to the morgue again. Unfortunately for them, the lowest-ranking person usually has to do the dirty work, but as often as they would let me, I would volunteer to either escort them or just take the deceased myself.

Chapter 5: The Pitfall of Perception

By this time, I was working out two times a day: once in the morning at the large fitness room at the medical center, and in the evenings when I was off work, I would lift weights at a large well-known health club. In the gym most people knew who I was, and as often as I could, I would talk and interact with pretty much everyone. However, they all knew that when I put my headphones on, they would need to leave me alone until after I was finished with my workout. I may not have been the biggest guy on the floor, but whether it was my size or strength, I stood out in the gym. For most people at the fitness center, it was more of a social gathering rather than a place to train your physical body, and when I was done with my workout, I would join in with their conversations. One of the things that always came naturally to me was the ability to listen to people; most people liked the fact that I had nowhere else to go after I took my protein shake.

Usually in the gym, I didn't see much by way of the spirit because I was too busy with my workout, but it was in the social times that things would appear. Often it would be a demonic spirit of deception, so I would try to end the conversation by saying, "Can I pray for you really quick?"

More often than not, when I would see the people again, they would say something like "I always feel better when I talk to you" or "You're a very good listener."

There was one particular person who worked in the fitness center nursery who would sometimes catch me on the way out the door. Our conversation was always the same, her husband didn't listen to anything she said, he traveled a lot with his job, and she had questions about whether he was being faithful to her. I made sure that we were always in a public place, sometimes in the fitness center and sometimes sitting on the hood of one of our cars; I didn't want anybody to get the wrong idea. I had said little prayers with her quite often, and sometimes I would place my hand on her shoulder while praying. I guess this led people to the wrong assumption as to what we were doing, but in truth there was really nothing happening between us at all.

Because of the sports teams that were in the area and the size of the gym, there were many professional athletes, both in baseball and football, who trained at this facility in their off-season. One of the professional football players was a friend of this lady's husband's. I had sensed in the spirit for some time what people were thinking, but I didn't have the heart to tell her that we should stop talking because of this. One day this professional football player, a very large offensive lineman, came up to me and told me that I needed to leave his friend's wife alone.

I said, "I agree, and I wish that your friend would either get a different job or possibly learn to just listen to his wife so I wouldn't have to."

Well, this made him pretty mad, and in the middle of the gym, he decided that we were going to have it out, I sensed that there wasn't much fear in him due to his large size, and I knew for a fact that I wasn't about to entertain any demonic entity of fear myself. So once again praying under my breath, I asked for peace in Jesus's name. He quickly asked me what it was I said under my breath, so I told him that I was just praying a short prayer because in truth, he and I were friends and had always gotten along before this moment. I told him that most of the time all I was doing with his friend's wife was allowing her to vent her frustrations and once in a while pray with her. Once the situation deescalated, we were able to talk and get to the truth of what was actually happening. But I learned an important lesson that day: regardless of what it is you are doing, there is always a perception of what people think is happening, and I would need to be more aware of this in the future.

One of my other friends, who was also a professional football player for the local team, said that they were looking for practice squad players and asked me if I might be interested because I had played some football here and there as well as some overseas. He gave me the information and told me where to go to sign up. It sounded like a chance to prove myself, being that I was told when I was overseas that I was physically incapable of performing my job. Maybe I was doing this for myself, or maybe I wanted to prove my naysayers wrong.

Back to the Basement

About that time at the medical center, they decided to move me from the fast pace of the ER to one of the slowest moving areas, the morgue. I didn't really like being down there when they would send me from the ER, and I would try to get back upstairs as soon as possible. I'm not really sure if it was because of what I could sense in the spirit or if it was just the smell, but either way this was not going to be easy for me. Sometimes the demonic entities would hang around the morgue like flies on the wall. I would cast them out, but the next day they would be there waiting for me. It was redundant, and at times I felt like I was walking in mud down there. It didn't help that the doctors who worked down there were slightly odd themselves.

The doctor would mark on the patient's chart as to the area on the body where I was to make cuts so they could examine the internal organs at a later time. I never actually opened up the deceased for the autopsies; the doctors did that. But I was always there to assist when they did the autopsies, usually just to discover the cause of death per a prior doctor's orders. In some cases, no one would come to claim the bodies from the morgue, so we would have to take the deceased individuals to be cremated. They would also have the bodies cremated if they had some sort of disease that was contagious. As you could guess, going to the crematorium was even worse than going down to the morgue; the crematorium to me always looked like some strange compartment of hell, and the old guy who ran the place looked like someone you would see in a horror movie. Back in my dungeon, or the morgue, it was always kept at about 47 degrees, so when you went from the crematorium to the morgue, I'm sure there was at least a 50-degree difference. It was a little depressing working down there, and I understood why they had to rotate staff in and out; I'm pretty sure if anybody stayed in there long enough, they would have pretty bad mental images on what you would see from day to day. On the spiritual side, I got to a point where I wouldn't even tell the demonic entities to leave because it was like an everyday event, and I started wondering what the purpose; they were going be back here again tomorrow.

Sometimes we would have guys who were in their twenties and thirties, and doing autopsies on them hit a little bit too close to home, but most of the time, the guys were older and in pretty rough shape. None of it was ever easy to do, and it felt like I was down there for years instead of just months. Because this medical center dealt exclusively with veterans, we very rarely saw any female patients. Maybe there were some on occasion, but to this point at the hospital, I don't remember seeing any in the morgue. Obviously, we didn't see any children either; this was probably a good thing because I don't think I would do very well working with children in this environment.

From the morgue they moved me back upstairs to an HIV/hepatitis B unit. In this unit we had to wear a special garment over our clothes as well as a mask to make sure we didn't breathe in anything we weren't supposed to, and we wore eye protection as well. The rooms with the hepatitis B patients had special purifiers in the room so that the air quality would stay at an acceptable level. I felt I was lucky because I was on the HIV side of the unit, and air quality wasn't really that big of a deal. We did have to be very careful with any blood samples or saliva samples, as well as any type of body fluids in general. Really if you followed all the hospital precautions, there was nothing to worry about, just taking care of people who were sick and trying to recover.

I didn't see as many angelic beings up there. In a lot of the rooms, the patients were dealing with one form of a demonic entity or another, and when I did see angels, I would ask the patients if they had a relationship with God. If not, I was sure one of their family members was praying for them.

Sometimes they would say things like, "I don't think anybody in my family is praying for me."

I would simply say, "I believe you're wrong; I think without a doubt there is somebody praying for you." Of course, I could never tell them why.

Some of the guys in the unit I would ask if they wanted me to pray with them. Most would say yes, but there were always the ones who would say that they didn't believe in that stuff. Under my breath I would pray a prayer for them anyway. I think whether people wanted to believe in God or didn't want to believe, God's presence was still there, and when I could try to bring them a message of hope and freedom from their afflictions, I would. It's always been interesting to me how, when people are at an extremely low point in their life more often than not, they will seek God. Usually the ones who don't seek God feel like they have done so many things wrong in their lives that he will never forgive them. My message to them was, "God so loved the world, that he gave his only son, and whosoever believes in him should not perish but have everlasting life" (John 3:16 KJV). I would also quote Matthew 7:7 (KJV): "Ask and it will be given to you; seek and you will find; knock and the door will be opened to you."

Around that same time, my friend who had asked me if I wanted to try out for the practice squad on the local football team was inquiring about my progress. I told him that I had talked to my supervisors at the medical center and they thought that it would work out fine due to the fact there were so many different shifts at the hospital. While I continued to work at the medical center, I tried out for this team. I was in pretty good shape but not in football shape—that is, I hadn't hit anyone (on a football field) or had been hit by anyone since the previous year playing football overseas. My friend at the gym met me at the facilities and prepared me for what I was about to encounter. He said that some of his teammates who worked out at the gym along with him would put in a good word, but the rest was up to me. We started out just doing basic football drills, nothing I hadn't done hundreds of times, and of course everyone who was walking into camp was confident as far as their chances on making the squad. I really wasn't worried because I was making money at the medical center. I also knew that practice squad players didn't make much money. Some of the men were trying out with hopes to make the active roster, and others of us just wanted to have fun and be able to say that we were given the chance to play professional football. For me it was just fun to get back to a game that I love to play, and in truth I would've played for free just to tackle someone again. I really didn't talk to anyone at all when I was there except for the one individual who had invited me. He told me I need to loosen up, but this was the only way I knew how to play the game; I was quiet and extremely focused. I had dropped my morning workout routine to make time for the tryouts, but I continued my weight training in the evening. I didn't really tell anyone what I was doing, I guess because that way, if I didn't make it, I wouldn't have to explain myself. The only ones who knew what I was doing were my medical center supervisors.

Before I knew it, they had suited us up in shoulder pads and helmets, but mostly we were hitting tackling dummies and coaches who were holding large pads. I noticed that as the weeks went by, the number of people who were trying out for the practice squad was shrinking. When I asked my friend about this, he enlightened me and said that if there is a red tag hanging in your locker after practice, you don't have to come back anymore. Now I was always worried that after practice, I, too, would have a red tag hanging in my locker to greet me. The truth was I enjoyed just being around the football team. When we finally started full contact in practice, I was beyond ready, and some of the people who were already on the team were not quite as ready to hit as I was. They had to pull me aside and explain how this whole thing worked. It went like this: they can hit you as hard as they want, but if you hit and hurt one of the signed contract players they won't even let you buy a ticket to watch the game from the seats, let alone letting you back on the practice field. What I decided was if I was given the opportunity to hit another practice squad player, I was going to do everything I could to prove my worth. I guess it worked because I never got a red tag. And yes, in the eighties, a practice squad player didn't make much money, but as I said before, I would've played for free if they wanted me to. One thing that always motivated me above all other things was people telling me that I wasn't capable of doing something. Maybe I just want to prove that I was still physically capable of doing anything in this world that I put my mind to.

Finding My Niche

At the medical center, once football season started, many of my coworkers acted like I was some type of celebrity. I did my best to explain to them that I was just a practice squad player, but from that moment on, they would introduce me as a player actually on the team. I knew that if they needed to bring me up to the game squad, they could, but that was only if they needed me. The team did allow me to play in some preseason games, and according to my friend who invited me to camp, I did a pretty good job. At the medical center, they decided to move me to a part of the hospital where I would be less likely to catch any viruses and get sick and not be able to play football: the psychiatric ward. It was on the top floor of the medical center, and as you walked up to the hospital from the parking lot, you would notice that the entire top floor had bars over the windows. Yes, it looked like some type of a prison up there.

From the first minute I walked into this gated unit, I realized that this was going to be like no other experience I'd ever had before. As a seer this was quite a sight to behold. I had been in alleged haunted houses that had less demonic entity than this. The only thing I could equate this to was maybe going to a horror movie at the theater, but not quite as spiritually concentrated.

As I walked into the unit, the charge nurse said to me, "Don't worry; you'll get used to this."

I said to myself, "I think that God had been preparing me for just this moment in time."

There were demonic entities everywhere, and the nursing staff was passing out different types of medication to most of the patients on the floor. The people working in the psychiatric ward had become immune to their surroundings. I found out very fast that my physical size was going to play a key role in working in this unit. It turned out that having twenty-one-inch biceps commanded some respect with patients who didn't notice many other things around them. They also thought that it was pretty cool that I was a military veteran like them. As for the demonic entities, they would play their little games with me to see if I could actually see where they were, once it was established that I could see them. They would say things like, "Seer, have you come to cast us out?"

The staff said that they only had a small number of people who were assigned to the psychiatric ward; the rest of the staff was rotated every two months or so. Some of the female nurses did very well up on this unit. It helped if they were tough and aggressive. But the smaller and more attractive they were, the harder the patients were on them. Some of the nurses stayed only one or two shifts.

After two or three weeks, the charge nurse came to me and said, "I hope you like it up here because we've asked for you to be permanently assigned to this unit."

I was happy about this; first, because I liked being up there, but secondly, I didn't really like moving around that much throughout the hospital. Most of the demonic entities that I would be dealing with were demons of deception, and there were a lot of patients who had been dealing with these problems for quite a while. Some of the entities were even entangled with the patient. Still not willing to ask any questions at my church, I would do my best to figure this out on my own. I was untrained as to how to use my gift and my authority and why it was that when I would cast out demonic entities, they would return the next day. All I could attribute this to was my own shortcomings because I knew it wasn't God's will for these people to be tortured like this. Angelic beings were a rarity on this floor, and most of my fellow nurses were not Christians. They were very good people but had no interest in what I had to say—"Just keep giving the shots and hand them pills"—so I did my job as I was told.

For the first month or so, I was just doing vitals, giving shots, and handing out medications. Most of these people had tried to commit suicide at some point, so there were many restrictions on this unit to keep them from possibly hurting themselves. We had a room that had two pool tables in it, but instead of having pool sticks made of wood and billiard balls that were hard, everything was made of a type of foam substance so patients couldn't hurt themselves or each other. Occasionally fights would break out in the pool room. It was one of the common areas, and for whatever reason, they thought the pool sticks were made out of wood and had the potential to inflict some pain—but nope, just foam. They would also go into the rooms and get their pillowcases and fill them with the billiard balls made of foam. I don't intend to sound mean, but it was a little comical to watch since everything they were using was made of foam. It turned out looking like a bad version of a pillow fight. The staff was made up mostly of male nurses/bouncers who would break up these supposed brawls, and no one was ever really hurt. From time to time, someone would get poked in the eye, but that was about it. Most of the patients knew they were dealing with foam and would laugh about it but did it anyway just to break up the monotony of living in what they called "the penthouse jail cell."

Chapter 6: Life Is Never Boring

I stayed busy with church, work, and football, probably so busy that I never really got involved with our church other than going to most of the services on Sunday nights. I had still never mentioned to anybody in the church or on the staff what I was watching in the spirit unfold each week in the services. They didn't talk much about the gifts of the spirit, and I didn't know their stance, so the best course of action for me was to just stay quiet. Some of the guys I played football with went to our church, but they tried to keep a low profile so they wouldn't draw much attention to themselves, and the pastor was very good about allowing them to stay out of the spotlight. Football went well, and in this first season, they had me suit up a couple of times and do some special-teams work on kickoffs or punt team. The family that owned the team was Christians, and it was very common for us to pray before practice as well as before games. I know that some of the people went through the motions because they were paid to do so, but I also know that anytime the word of God is spoken, it never comes back void. Even though there was some rough locker room talk and sideline talk, as happens with any sports or football team, I always sensed the presence of God. I knew that at least part of the football team attended church on a regular basis, usually during evening services on Sunday or Friday nights. We would often have different local pastors come in to give us a short word and pray over us. I had my own unique way of looking at these little miniservices before games. In my mind I felt that the Roman gladiators had received similar prayers and words before they went off to do battle. Once most of the guys had accepted me, I was able to give them spiritual words of encouragement for both on and off the field. At times God would give me insight as to what they were dealing with and would allow me to minister to them using his words. At times they would refer to me as the "fist of God," both on and off the field, and they enjoyed it when the coaches would allow me to suit up and play. By this time, I had put on quite a bit more muscle weight and at six-feet-one, I weighed in at about 245 pounds, or at least that's what they would announce me as.

Dealing with Demons

At the medical center, things were never boring, and every time I would show up for my shift, the demonic entities would, in their own ways greet me at the door. (Not really; it just felt that way.) Most of the patients in this unit were actually OK with being here because, in most cases, the alternative was doing jail or prison time for one reason or another. At least here they knew they would have company as well as a warm bed and three meals a day. As I said before, we were always dealing with demons of deception that would constantly come in and convince them that it was better to just end their lives. Some of the precautions we had to take were with razor blades. We only had electric razors, so from time to time, you would hear a buzzing sound in their bedrooms, only to walk in and see them with an electric razor going up and down the wrist and forearm. As I would walk in on them, I would cast off the demon and then make a comment as to how clean shaven their wrist and forearm was going to be for the next few days. Between the medications and the demonic deception, they were unaware that the electric razor was not able to penetrate their skin. We also had showerheads and shower rods that would break away very easily because some of the patients would try to hang themselves using different items for rope. As sad as it sounds, we always knew when this was happening because the patient would come out of the shower with a bruised knee and a limp.

I would ask my guys, "Did you forget that those things will break away if you put any of your body weight on them?"

I would then cast out whatever demon they were dealing with at that time, and we would usually sit down and talk. One of the other problems we would have to deal with was that when they came into the ward, they were often under the influence of a multitude of drugs. They would even eat sterno (a type of accelerant) or even drink gasoline when they couldn't get ahold of actual alcohol or drugs.

Demonic entities were always present when they would come into our unit. Sometimes multiple demons would be crawling on them and even protruding from their body. In the hectic moments that would ensue after they arrived, I would do my best to bind these demons under my breath while the police officers as well as the nursing staff would unfortunately put them in an isolation room. If they were too combative, we would even have to strap them down on a table for short periods of time so that they wouldn't hurt themselves or anyone else. They would allow me to go into the isolation room on a regular basis to try to talk them down, as well as to see if the medications that we would administer were taking effect. Seeing in the spirit was quite effective in these times because they would try to tell you, "I'm OK; let me up," and I would be able to see the demonic entity speaking to them. Sometimes I would fall for it and release their hands so they could get a drink of water or something, and often they would lunge at me and try to grab at my clothes. You only get fooled a couple of times before you realize that until the demonic entity leaves their presence, it's hard to believe anything they say is true.

There were always cameras and microphones in the room, so I would have to be careful as to how I handled the situation. The doctors and most of the nurses were convinced that medicating them was the only process to calm them down, so I would keep a very low profile when trying to cast out these demons that were with these new patients coming into our unit. Once they were in the unit long enough and doing well with their medications, they were allowed to go down to the gift shop in the medical center and were always escorted by the nursing staff as well as hospital security. They were able to buy much of what they wanted, but many times they would try to purchase items that they were not allowed to have so that they could use them for trade up on the unit. One such item was mouthwash. As harmless as that may seem for them, that was almost as good as getting a bottle of hard liquor, and they would try to buy the biggest bottle in the store. Some of the cashiers knew the items they were not allowed to purchase, and some just didn't care. From time to time, some of these items would actually make it upstairs—not by way of a bag, but they would usually stuff it in some part of their clothing. It was always a risk because if they got caught with it, they wouldn't be able to go down to the gift shop for quite some time.

Cigarettes were always a very big trade item on our floor and were used a little like currency.

Most of the patients during mealtimes would eat in the dining room, but some, due to inability or combativeness, were unable to eat with the general population of the patients. They were given their meals in their rooms until they were able to join the rest of the patients. In the dining facility, they were only allowed to have foam plates and plastic spoons and forks; no plastic knives were allowed. And as you probably guessed, once in a while, we would have physical altercations during mealtime. Sometimes the patients would take sides, and we would have to do our best to keep everything as calm as possible; usually removing one of the patients was the best course of action. Seeing in the spirit most of the time on this unit was an advantage, but sometimes I would get busy doing my work and not pay attention as to what the entities were doing. The supernatural presence was pretty much always there, and the patients often just allowed them to get into their heads because it was what they had always done. There were the occasions when I would pick up on things that the patients were planning, sometimes when they would have extracurricular activities (fights) planned before they even entered the dining room. I know this sounds bad, but it looked like a cheesy fight scene from a low-budget movie using plastic spoons and forks as weapons. Because I was an ex-bouncer, it was generally easy to deescalate and remove the individuals who had instigated the uprising. But there was the one time that I did get stabbed in the back of my shoulder with a plastic fork trying to keep one of the patients from getting hurt. When I turned around, I saw it was one of my patients who were known for practicing cannibalism. He said, "Sorry, man," and then proceeded to lick the fork.

This particular patient was actually one of my favorite guys in the unit. He was a little taller than me with a medium build. He had been sent as a soldier in an earlier war and had gotten separated from his unit for quite some time, and to survive, he had resorted to cannibalism. He was very well mannered and most of the time kept his hair in a long ponytail. Most of the nursing staff liked him, but he would try to lull you into a sense of complacency as to what his intentions were.

One time when he was assigned to a new nurse up on the unit, he talked them into taking him down to the gift shop, and even with hospital security there, he was able to give them the slip and make his way out of the hospital and back on the streets. He was of special interest to the police because for the most part, it was easier for him to dine on unsuspecting civilians who also lived on the streets than it was to steal food or beg for a handout.

An Evening at the Bus Station

One evening several weeks after he liberated himself from our unit, I was coming on for my shift, and there were a few police officers waiting for me at the nurse's desk. They asked my charge nurse if we could go into a room and talk. Of course my charge nurse and I were happy to oblige. Once in the room, they explained to us that my patient who had escaped from the medical center was holed up in a bus station and that the police were in a type of standoff with him. My patient had requested that I be brought in as a mediator, and he assured them that he would talk to me. Into the squad car I went to go downtown and have a talk with him.

When we arrived at the bus station, they brought me in to an area where people were able to rent large lockers to store luggage. They had been doing some construction on the building, and my patient was able to commandeer a hacksaw and some blades and had somehow gotten the keys to several of the lockers all in a row. Using the hacksaw and blades, he had cut out the walls that separated the lockers; due to the construction, no one had noticed the additional noise as he constructed his small home. Some of the construction workers even thought he was one of them and paid him no attention. He had kept all the keys to the lockers and, from the inside, was able to go in or out any of the large locker doors. He had also bent some of the louvers on the doors so that he was able to look out into the bus station, so people would hopefully not see him coming and going. It must've worked well for a while, but then I guess someone noticed him hanging around the bus station and wasn't sure who he was or where he was going and eventually was able to figure it out. Then the police were notified, and after they identified him, they became worried as to what he had been doing. The officer in charge asked me how I wanted to handle this.

I said, "I guess I'll just walk up and knock on his locker door."

The police officer said, "That's it?"

I said, "Well, it sounds good to me."

So off I went walking toward the lockers. As I approached them, my patient yelled out to me what number locker to come to, I guess indicating that this was his front door. Just before I reached the locker door, it opened about an inch or two, and I heard a familiar voice say, "Come on in, man."

I opened the door and ducked a little bit to go in. I was surprised at how large these lockers actually were. I was a fairly decent-size guy, and I was able to stand inside with plenty of room for my shoulders, but I did have to duck just a little bit. There was a strange smell that obviously I did not mention, and the fact that there were several demonic entities in this small space with him. I asked him if he would object if I did some spiritual housecleaning before we talked, and he said, "Sure, go ahead."

So I prayed. He was pretty much in his right mind as we began our conversation. He asked me what I thought of his place. I said it looked a lot bigger on the inside than it did on the outside. He smiled and said, "I knew you would like it."

He asked me if he was going to have to go to jail or if he could go back to the psychiatric ward. He said, "I haven't eaten anybody. These vending machines around here are easy to get into if you have the right equipment."

I asked him, "Why didn't they just come in here and get you?"

He said that he had convinced the people who ran the bus station that he had a bomb or some type of weapon, and they really didn't want to get any closer.

I said, "I'm guessing you don't have anything?"

He said, "No, I just want them to keep their distance."

I said, "OK, let me go out and talk to them for a minute and see if they will agree to let you come back to the psychiatric hospital with me, and try to keep your spiritual friends from returning until after I get back."

He smiled and said, "I'll try."

I went out to speak with the police. They said that except for some destruction of private property, they really didn't have any charges against him, and it would be fine if I took him back to the psychiatric ward to be readmitted into the unit.

I told them, "As long as you allow me to stay with him, I think everything will be fine, and to my knowledge, there is no bomb or weapon in the storage lockers, but I guess you'll have to check that out a little more after I get him off the premises."

I walked back to the lockers and my patient, just like before, popped the door open as I approached. He asked about what they had said. I told him as long as he was nice and went back to the psychiatric ward with me, everything should be fine.

I said "Now when we leave are, they aren't going to find anything in the lockers that you haven't told me about?"

He said, "Nope, and they are welcome to eat the vending machine food that I have stockpiled in the box."

I asked, "Do you have any clothes or anything you want to take with you?"

He said, "I've packed a couple boxes, and I'm ready to go."

With that, I walked out from the lockers in front of him, and written on the box with a marker were the words "Not a bomb." As the policeman came up to greet us, we stopped and put the boxes on the ground, and they proceeded to check my patient for any weapons as well as the boxes we were carrying. When everything was cleared, they went to his lockers to make sure there wasn't anything of a destructive nature in his newly remodeled habitat. Afterward they were nice enough to give us a ride back to the medical center and an escort back onto the psychiatric ward.

As we got him checked back into the unit, he said to me, "Thanks for coming and getting me from the bus station, and by the way sorry, again for stabbing you in the shoulder with that plastic fork."

Not all of the patients on the ward were easy to get along with. In some cases, you couldn't turn your back on them because they were looking for an opportunity to possibly acquire a hostage or whoever seemed to be in charge, usually because they wanted access to more drugs or they just wanted out of the unit. We had one patient that for whatever reason thought he was a famous singer from the late fifties and sixties. He was a short, stocky guy who wore his hair in a type of a pompadour and had large pork chop sideburns; he also had a tattoo of a swastika on his forehead. He was often the focal point of many of the disputes on the ward and sometimes was put into restraints due to his combativeness. This particular patient was never assigned to me, and I never learned much about him. What I did know was that the demonic entity that controlled and tormented him was never far away and would often put him in situations where the outcome for this particular patient was not going to be good. Everyone in the unit was trained in some form of martial arts, not so much so we could injure anyone, but mostly so that we could control a situation until help would arrive. Most of us became good at subduing attackers because on the unit, we got to practice it almost on a daily basis in real-world situations. Luckily, most of the patients who were assigned to us became familiar, and we would learn how to keep them calm, which in turn would make our jobs a lot easier.

Chapter 7: Rubber-Band Girl

I had met a girl at the gym, and she appeared to be chasing me. Since I didn't like going to dinner or movies by myself, and she often invited herself, we started hanging out. Most of the time, I would try to involve other people when we went out so that it didn't look like it was exclusive, and sometimes we would double date with her roommate or someone else. She was only interested in the fact that I played football and that I was big enough to get noticed when we went places. Occasionally I would go to her apartment to pick her up, and she would invite me in. I noticed that she had pictures of old boyfriends who also lifted weights and were bigger than average. To me it was a little bit strange to have these pictures of people that she used to date, but because I wasn't all that serious in the relationship, I never mentioned anything. I also noticed her roommate was from the same small Midwest town that she was from. Her roommate later in the year would be going into the military, so she was just staying there until she left for basic training.

One time her roommate came to the gym and asked my workout partner if we had a rubber band for her hair. I looked at her like she was a little bit crazy and said, "No, we don't have a rubber band."

My workout partner (who, by the way, had no hair), said, "Yes, I have a rubber band." He handed her a rubber band off his wrist.

I gave him a dumb look as if to say, "Why in the world would you have a rubber band?" He gave the rubber band to the roommate of the girl I was seeing, and after that encounter, they would always talk when she was at the gym. I told my workout partner that maybe we should go on a double date together and he could take out the rubber-band girl because I was dating her roommate. I believe he asked her out on several occasions, but for whatever reason she was never interested. On many other occasions, the girl I was seeing and her roommate, the rubber-band girl, went on other double dates together. At one point the girl I was seeing had mentioned to her roommate that she was getting serious with me. The roommate, knowing that I was not serious at all with her friend, decided to make me aware of her roommate's feelings toward me. I may have panicked a little bit because this was never my intention, but I was thankful for the information that was given to me. After that I did my best to spend less and less time with this girl from the gym and told her on several occasions that we were just friends. According to the roommate, she wasn't getting the hint and was still planning her future that included me.

Demigod

By this time at the medical center, I'd had my own patients for quite a while now. Some would come and go, only staying long enough to get better and then would be released back to their families. But some would stay for long periods of time, and you would get to know these patients very well—so well that you would remember them forever, like they were a friend from your past. This was one of those patients. If I am honest, he was one of my favorites; he never really tried to hurt anyone but was very confused as to who he was and what he was supposed to do. In the military he had suffered some type of head injury but had no scars from the incident that I knew of. But in his mind, he was a demigod, which at least in his mind gave him the ability to levitate very large objects or move them from one place to another. In the natural as well as the supernatural, I had seen this done many times in my life, so I knew that if the demonic entities were willing to, they did possess the power to move objects. But in this particular patient's case, some of the objects that he wanted to move were quite large, like trees that were planted in the ground or vehicles in the parking lot that we could see from our window at the top of the medical center. At one point he and I were looking out the window, and he told me to watch a certain tree off in the distance. I'm pretty sure I was looking at the right tree, and in his mind the tree was several feet off the ground; either I wasn't seeing exactly what he was seeing or I had the wrong tree. In either case I never saw a tree levitate, nor with this particular self-proclaimed demigod did I ever see him pick up and move a car from one place to the next. One time I did see him attempt to shape-shift himself so that he would fit through the bars on the top floor of the medical center; he was going to levitate himself outside the window and escape. He was convinced that he could do this, and I'm pretty sure that the multiple demonic entities that were speaking to him had him convinced him of this, but in the natural, all that happened was that he got his head stuck in the bars of the window, and we had to soap up his head in order to slide it out of the bars.

He also tried to convince me that he had the power to make me a demigod as well and that I would be able to move objects someday as well as he did. Little did he know that when I was a kid, I was allowed to do those things as well, but I was no demigod. As odd as the conversation was, he would even have arguments with other patients in the psychiatric ward about his abilities; some of the patients would say things like, "I know I'm crazy, but you're a special kind of crazy."

Sometimes the patient's doctors would allow them to go to the local baseball games; the baseball team would donate tickets to the hospital so that patients who were healthy enough to watch the game could go for free. Usually it was on a Tuesday or Wednesday game when they didn't have a lot of people coming to the stadium. The seats were often out in the middle of nowhere because they didn't want our patients interacting with their paying baseball fans.

On one such trip, I was able to take four of my patients, and they were allowed to wear their street clothes instead of our hospital jumpsuits, but they were all attached to each other by the waist with a type of belt restraint that connected them. It was loose enough that they could turn all the way around but attached so that if they decided to run, they would have to do it in perfect unison—and let's face it, that was never going to happen. My patient who thought he was a demigod was in my group. Three of my other patients would complain because they had to be attached to him for the entire ride over, as well as through the entire game and on the bus ride back, but they endured this because they wanted to get out of the hospital for a while and watch a live baseball game.

The cannibal patient I mentioned earlier made comments like, "You make us crazy people look bad," and "If they give me enough cheese dip, I may just take bites out of you during the game."

My demigod patient would answer him, saying, "You know it's bad luck to eat a demigod, don't you?"

He answered, "I live in a psychiatric hospital. How much more bad luck is there for me?"

As a seer, I felt this was all a cross between being spiritually unfortunate and spiritually entertaining, depending on how you looked at it. Generally, I would cast them out, but there was always one demonic entity that was not far away, and the patients would invite them back in from one moment to the next. This was my constant dilemma, and I have to admit, at times I would get frustrated and give up, sit back, and watch the show that was going on in the spiritual between my patients.

At this particular baseball game, there were three groups of patients from the psychiatric unit, and each group had a nurse with them as well as hospital security. Now my patient who thought he was a demigod had an unusual haircut. It was basically an Afro that was shaved on the sides and formed what looked like a stovepipe on top of his head, and it was flat on the top. So when he was sitting in the stadium seats, the patient who was seated behind him used the top of his hair as a small table for his nachos and cheese dip, much to the delight of the other patients. This self-proclaimed demigod unfortunately had a particular player on the baseball team whom he really liked, so every time he would come up to the plate to bat, he would stand up, but before he did, the patient who was behind him would have to remove his food. The entertaining part about this was that every time he would stand up, the other three patients would have to stand up as well, making for a small wave that no one joined in with.

When this particular player would come to the plate, our demigod would stand up and put what we called a "whammy" on him, and with that he was supposed to be able to hit the ball that much farther. Unfortunately, it seemed to have quite the opposite effect on this particular baseball player, because every time he would stand up and do this, the player would strike out. The other patients decided that it was his fault that this player was striking out, but our demigod assured them that he was doing everything right and it wasn't his fault. Finally, the last time this player came to bat, they held our demigod down in his seat, and as you can probably guess, he proceeded to hit the ball out of the park, winning the game for the home team. Our demigod explained himself by saying he was just trying to make the game interesting and that he knew that was going to happen all along. Even the patients from the psychiatric ward questioned his abilities and came to the conclusion that he lived in his own special world.

Girl in the Mix

By this time, even though I was a self-proclaimed official bachelor, I was spending more time with my girlfriend's roommate, talking about pretty much everything. She didn't seem to care that I played football or that I was a nurse at the medical center, and I don't think she liked the fact that I was bigger than most of the guys in any room or the gym we worked out in. Besides all that, she had a basic training date and was going into the military that fall. She was really just counting the days and weeks until she left for training. Her roommate, who was by this time my ex-girlfriend, had told her it was OK to date me since we had become such good friends. The girl, whom I had at one time called "the rubber-band girl," was spending more and more time with me. We liked most of the same things, and the fact that I could give her insight on basic training and life in the military was a topic that she was interested in hearing about.

She came from a large family in a small town, and they were all very close knit. My upbringing was quite the opposite, so to me it was fascinating talking to someone who was raised in such a different environment from me. I knew we had made a connection, but she would be leaving in the fall, and it was more than likely I wouldn't see her again after she went to basic training. Morning football practices had begun, and I was trying to prepare myself for whatever they were going to have me do in the upcoming season. As a practice squad player at this time, I was only required to go to the morning sessions, and after that, I would go to work and then later to the gym for weight training.

As always, going to work was never boring or mundane; it was very rare that we had a female patient come into our psychiatric ward. The guys were easier to handle because they knew that physically speaking, there was going to be no competition between them and me. A woman was committed into the psychiatric hospital and was a lot less intimidated by my size. She had her own small unit, and it was several weeks before we could even allow her to mix with our male-dominated general population. In the spiritual, the demonic entities that were constantly moving about at her feet were common to me, but there was one demonic entity that was less familiar. This particular demon would cause her to say things and make gestures that were hard for most guys to not pay attention to. It seemed to crave physical contact and would try to invite you in to have relations with it.

The first time I was introduced to this new patient, two of the demons at her feet looked at me and then quickly climbed up her side and started repeating, "Can you see me? I think he can see us."

The first words she ever said to me were, "My demons like you. Or do they?"

It was a constant struggle for the other patients in the unit because they knew she had been admitted and wanted us to release her into the main part of the unit. My vote was that it was a bad idea. Luckily, we had female charge nurses on the ward as well, but this patient would often get very violent, so as a rule, we would have to take care of this patient in pairs. Most of the female nurses could handle themselves just fine, and when this particular patient felt that she was unable to be violent with them, she would resort back to being promiscuous. Either way you looked at it, it was a slippery slope. The lesser demonic entities were easy to cast out on a daily basis, but the one more dominant demon had a strong grasp on this particular patient and would often just move out of the way and sit in the corner of the room. I have no doubt that God had given me the ability to cast this demonic entity out, so I'm sure the problem wasn't God; the problem was I didn't feel confident enough as a Christian, and the fact that she would continually invite this entity back into her presence.

When I was able to, I would talk to her about God, and she would laugh at me, saying that she didn't need my God, that she had a god of her own that she could have fun with and that this god of hers would have physical relations with her. I'm pretty sure that this demonic entity would manifest to her as a man and would in some way have relations with her; I never knew this to be the truth firsthand, but in the spirit, I sensed this is what was happening. In my past I had seen demonic entities manifest into several different figures, so I knew this was something that, if the individual allowed it, could take place. It was only after several weeks that we would allow her into the general population of our unit and only for a short period of time, always escorted by one of the nursing staff. She enjoyed the fact that every time she was in the presence of the other patients, she would cause a great stir, and often fights would break out trying to get her attention. Later, when they realized that this patient was going to be long term, they moved her to a civilian female psychiatric hospital at a different location. Most of the guys in the unit were heartbroken because other than the female nurses in the unit, they didn't come in contact with a whole lot of women, and I am certain that none of the female nurses ever had any thoughts about making advances to any of our patients.

Twenty-Twenty

I continued to lift weights with one of my linebacker friends from the football team, and he would help me a great deal in gaining strength that I was previously unable to tap into. Football was going well for me, and I was able to suit up just like one of the signed players in many of the games. This, too, I kept to myself and didn't let on to any of my family members know who were football fans of this particular team. I was used to keeping things quiet. It was what I had always known as a seer, and this wasn't a whole lot different. I knew that people would view me as being crazy, a grown man with imaginary friends, and in football I didn't want to be seen as a failure. I was very familiar with failure. I felt as if I had failed my family, failed in baseball, failed in school and in college. I had failed to fulfill what I was trained to do in the military. I was an on-again-off-again football player, but in my eyes the fewer people that knew of my failures, the fewer people who could point fingers at me down the road. It sounds strange, but I knew that my God did not see me as a failure. I believe that in his eyes I was being fine-tuned and sharpened, preparing me for things that had yet to come in my life. The things that I saw as failures he saw as seasons of growth so that I would be able to withstand whatever it was in my future, the storms that life throws at me. Without a strong foundation based on God's word, survival for me was uncertain.

One thing that I had gotten good at was ignoring things that were going on around me in the supernatural; it wasn't like I saw in the spirit all the time, but I did without question most of the time. Rather than focusing on things that were in my peripheral vision, I would concentrate on things that were straight ahead of me. I got to the point where I could ignore things and not turn my head every five minutes or so, kind of like seeing somebody steal something and turning a blind eye and walking away. It was probably not the best way to overcome what was my own private dilemma, but without an owner's manual for seeing in the spirit, it was the best I could do. The fact was that if my walk with God had been stronger at this time, like when I was first saved at the church in Southern California, I have no doubt that God would've filtered what I see as he does now, but hindsight is always twenty-twenty.

Great Escape

By summertime my ex-girlfriend, her roommate, and I would still hang out from time to time, even watching fireworks together on the Fourth of July. They had been friends since childhood, and I suppose in their minds they weren't going to stop being friends because of a guy, which was good because I still liked hanging out with them, I just liked hanging out with the rubber-band girl more.

After the Fourth of July, we talked and defined what our relationship was, and our conclusion was that we were now boyfriend and girlfriend. The problem was my new girlfriend was going into the military in the next few months, but in our minds, we would just make the best of it and see how much contact we had with each other after all of her training was finished.

I knew that she was a Christian, but I also knew that we saw things much differently. She was from a small town and had grown up in a smaller church, and I was from the big city and the only church I knew was extremely large. We both loved God, and with an unforeseeable future in front of us, we decided to move forward as I did with most things one day at a time.

If being at the medical center did nothing else for me, it allowed me to be very aware of demonic entities and the ways that they would whisper into people's ears, most of the time making the person feel that it was their own thoughts. Sometimes I would see patients slapping their own head or face, as if trying to get these thoughts to physically move away from them. It was easy to give them temporary relief by casting out the demonic entities, but the other staff was convinced that the best way was shots or pills. Many times after they would be sedated, I would cast out demons that would be pushing on different parts of their head trying to create pain, but it was like an old friend that you knew without a doubt was bad for you but you always allowed them back in. We are of course creatures of habit; it's easy to say that we are to learn from our mistakes and do our best not to repeat them, but it's a whole different subject to actually walk that out. The strange thing was most of my patients felt as if I had some sort of unfair advantage over the other nursing staff. On a daily basis, I would tell my patients, "I'm not 100 percent sure what you're thinking, but whatever it is, I highly suggest you put those thoughts out of your mind." I wasn't able to hear what the demonic entities were saying to them; I just knew they were saying something, and it probably wasn't good.

Sometimes they would look at me and say, "OK, what am I thinking?" and in truth I would say, "I have no idea."

With that they would reply, "We may be in a mental hospital, but we're not stupid, and we don't know how you do it, but we are all pretty sure you have an idea of what it is we are thinking."

I just knew something was being said, and because of the source it was coming from, I knew that it probably would be mischievous or something that would get the patient in some sort of trouble.

One afternoon we were taking some of the patients outside of the hospital in a large grassy area on the medical center property. There were benches and trees, a place where they could get fresh air and feel like they weren't confined to the top floor of the hospital—although they would all bring their cigarettes; I would have to stand upwind because I've never liked the smell of any kind of smoke. I liked being out here in the sunshine and the light because it was like the demonic entities were far less active in this setting. We would laugh and talk among ourselves in regular conversation. Anytime we left the hospital, the patients were connected at the waist with a harness. You would've thought that with them all being prior military, they would be able to walk or even take off running in unison like all military soldiers have been trained to do, and on occasion, mostly just for laughs, they would try. In truth it was a poor attempt at a breakout, and the newer staff members would panic and jog after them. The security and staff members would just sit and continue our conversation as if nothing was happening, because we'd seen this attempted many times and had never seen it done successfully. They had trouble walking together, let alone when they would take off running and try to sound off some sort of cadence. Whether it was too many years out of the military or the fact they were all in pretty terrible shape, it was a form of entertainment for them. Within the first fifty feet, one or more would get out of step and get tangled up, and down they would go like a well-placed ball in a bowling alley.

Then they would get up, point fingers at each other, and cuss a lot.

Sometimes laughing, we would walk up to them and say, “Well, it’s a good thing you got some exercise today. Let’s go back to the ward.”

Of course, they would talk us into staying out a bit longer so that they could smoke some more cigarettes. We would generally let them because we liked being outside just as much as the patients did.

Girlfriend, Football, Hospital, and Secrets

This year I would suit up for more football games than any season before. Most of the time, it was just in case there was an injury and they would need me to fill in. At other times it was a kickoff team or punt team, and being a practice squad player made me very expendable. We had a much better season this particular year than we did the year before. I wasn’t a big fan of the coach, but who was I to argue? They were allowing me to put on a uniform and paying me a couple of bucks to hit some people, so I couldn’t complain at all. The good thing was that I only had to report for morning practices, and if they felt that I was going to suit up, usually for home games, I would have to go watch films on Fridays. Luckily for me, my brother (who was my roommate) didn’t ask very many questions. We had our own lives, and when we had the chance we would hang out, but with my job at the medical center, my girlfriend, and a part-time job playing ball, it didn't leave me a lot of time. Most of my extra time was spent with my girlfriend. When the season started, my girlfriend had left and was off to the military, giving me a lot of time to focus on work, football, and training. She had said that we would keep in touch, but I never really knew if that was going to happen or not. It wasn't as if I could pick up a phone anytime I wanted and just call her. The call had to be initiated on her end only when the training instructors (TIs) would allow her or the rest of the trainees to make phone calls. I had already been through basic military training, and I knew there was the possibility of her finding a replacement for me while she was there. But we did keep in contact, as much as she could while being in basic training. I even took a week off to go down and watch her graduate before she went off to her training school. Most of the time when couples get split up, they find out what the relationship is actually made of, and in this case, we grew quite a bit stronger. It was at this time that we first talked about the possibility of us getting married.

When I got home from the trip down to see my girlfriend graduate from basic training, things fell into place pretty quickly. In football we didn't play a lot of postseason games, so that was starting to wind down. It would be a tough to leave my brother, who had been my roommate for quite some time, as well as my job at the medical center, but when the angel had spoken to me when I was in the gym in Germany, he said that God would be taking me into a dry place, a desert, and it would be there that I would be given instructions. I didn't know where life was taking me, but I knew the city in the Midwest was not going to be my final destination. It was not my desert, and with that, I prayed and trusted God in this relationship as well as my future.

Chapter 8: Taking Me to the Desert

I had never shared with anyone—not my dad or my mom, my brothers or my sisters, or even my girlfriend, who was now my fiancée—that the supernatural realm was somehow open to me. I also knew that I was in a place in my life where I was at a spiritual standstill. With my brother and my coworkers as well as my teammates, I was never expected to achieve anything for the kingdom of God or the body of Christ. I also knew that I would have to deal with my own demons and keep them at bay as well as whatever demons my new fiancé was dealing with. I wondered if I was strong enough in the Lord to take on such a challenge. I was, without a doubt, ready to put everything on the line to see if there was more in my life than just the military, my work at the medical center, or my on-again off-again practice team participation. God had to have more for me; I was sure that the final page in my book that was written before I was born did not end here. Risking everything, I trusted this person that God had put in my life to allow me to grow in the word as well as in the spirit. My hope was that at some point I would be able to share with her my spiritual gift and that she would believe that I was not crazy. In the natural, I felt it was time to just trust God.

My fiancée and I, for the next few months, would do our best to plan a wedding that would land between her graduating from military training school and her first duty assignment, wherever that would be. I also packed up whatever household goods I had and put in my notice with the medical center that I would be leaving in the coming months; my brother was very understanding and helped me as much as he could.

This was an incredible leap of faith, one that was going to affect a lot of people. Some were friends, some were coworkers, and then there was my family, but I also knew that I was removing a great deal of distractions, which would allow me to focus on my new wife and an elevated walk with God. I also knew that my fiancée and I would face many struggles, and we would have to grow together as a newly married couple but more so in our relationship with God.

Shortly after arriving at her training school, my fiancée received orders to her duty assignment that she would report to after completing school, and, as God had spoken to me while I was still in Germany, we were to go to the high plains into the desert of New Mexico. It was at that time that I was sure this was God. In my eyes God had led many great men of the Bible into the desert to teach them and show them the way that they were to go, and I felt confident that this new life in front of me was confirmation that I was going the right direction. As my fiancée and I researched the location that would be our new home, we actually became confused because our assumption was that we would be somewhere near a larger city in New Mexico. Having trouble locating exactly where it was on a map, we looked at the country of Mexico, thinking that maybe it was possible we had a new base in our southern neighbor. Technology wasn't what it is now at that time, so trying to find small towns on maps was often difficult. When we finally located where we were going, my fiancée was happy because to her, it was a much bigger city than where she was raised. But to me it was in the middle of nowhere, and I thought to myself that at least there would be few distractions other than my new wife, weight lifting, and church. There wasn't much else around the area, and again it was like what the angel had told me: God would take me into the desert. Well, we got that one right.

The wedding was strategically placed between my fiancée graduating from her training school and her reporting date to show up at her first duty assignment in New Mexico. The morning of our wedding day, my fiancée borrowed her dad's Pontiac station wagon to go find flowers for the wedding, and it just so happened that she rear-ended the back of a large four-wheel-drive truck and totaled the car. The funny thing was, her dad wasn't mad, but he did give us the car as a wedding gift for me to repair. I'm sure that should've been some sort of sign as to what I was in for the rest of this relationship, but just as everything else I've ever done in my life, I felt as if I could fix it and move on as I always had. It was a small wedding with family members only and was performed in the basement of a church in the Midwest; the minister who married us was a friend of my new wife's family. In truth I didn't know him very well, but he seemed to me like a wonderful older gentleman whom I felt truly loved God. Our wedding colors were light blue and white, possibly because I was former air force and my new bride was just starting her career in the air force. It was unlike weddings in this day and age, because I'm pretty sure the entire service cost us less than $100, but it was legal, and now I had gone full circle as far as the military was concerned. I had been a dependent child under my stepdad, I had been active duty military stationed in Germany, and now I was a dependent husband—a little funny if you think about it because when I was in high school, debating what I wanted to do for the rest of my life, being in the military fell far from the top of my list. Now looking back, I see the two constants in my life to this day have been God and the military. My dad was former navy during World War II, my father-in-law was former army during the Korean War, my stepdad was former air force during Desert Shield, and I was air force throughout the latter part of the Cold War—and now my wife was air force as well. I have no question that our families served our country well, and we continue to do so.

New Beginnings

The move to our first apartment was great. I drove a rented truck from where we had met and married down to our new duty assignment in the high plains of the desert. This was all new country to me, and the first thing that I noticed was that you could see for miles and miles with no obstructions, no mountains, and no trees—just open spaces. I arrived at the first of the year, and it was surprisingly cold, frozen, and snowy. It wasn't what I had expected coming to a desert, but the elevation was over four thousand feet. Our apartment was small, but we didn't care because we were both starting a brand-new adventure. I think my wife had a lot more to deal with than I did because she was starting a new base with new supervisors and a new husband. This was a lot to deal with for a young newly married military member, and I tried to help any way I could.

I had repaired the Pontiac station wagon that was wrecked the day of our wedding and sold my cars before coming down, so the station wagon was the only car that was brought to New Mexico. It was rather old with wood-looking paneling on the sides; my new bride and I were cruising in style, like driving a land yacht with room for ten. There was no question as to where the groceries were going to go because we had plenty of room. I decided to get a job at a local nursing home because of my nursing background, and I was pretty sure I could get hired quickly. I was familiar with working in nursing homes and briefly had worked in one before, as well as doing some of my clinical work there. As in any other type of work, you had two types of people working in nursing homes: the ones who actually loved being around the elderly and the ones who were just there to get a paycheck. In the spirit it was very easy to determine which one was which, and some of the nursing assistants were just there to check the boxes and go on without actually caring at all for the human being who was in front of them. The thing I loved about the nursing home was that almost every patient had an incredible story to tell if someone would just take the time to listen. I guess I've always loved history, so hearing them tell stories about themselves from an era long ago was fascinating to me, and the ones that could no longer tell their own story due to loss of memory were like pages taken from a book that could never be read again. Not all of the patients had angelic beings with them; some, like in the psychiatric ward, dealt with a type of demon of deception and bitterness like luggage they had carried around for far too long. Most of the time, the gruff ones didn't want to hear what I had to say about God and forgiveness, they were already set on the fact that you could never teach an old dog a new trick. On occasion, if I was persistent, reintroducing them to a walk with God was possible. I felt that as long as I was going to be here, I would do whatever I could to make sure that when their day came to meet the Lord, they had a proper introduction. Everything after that was simply between them and God.

The hardest thing about this type of work was that the staff members who were just doing a job could really not have cared less about the person that they were working with, especially when they took shortcuts, and sometimes were a little rough with them. The patients in the nursing home knew exactly who was who; to them it was no secret as to who really cared and who was there just to do a job.

Finding a Place to Worship

Very soon after arriving at our new base, we took on the task of finding a church. I knew what kind of church I was looking for, but I felt it was more important for my wife to find a church that she was comfortable with. I had never been to a small church where everyone knew everything about everyone else, but I was willing to give it a try. I was still pretty young in my Christian walk and didn't really know much about denominations and how different churches looked at the word of God. The way I was taught was that the Bible is the written word of God, and if the Bible says it, then that's what it is. I never really thought about people interpreting the word of God differently; let's face it—I'd only actually been a member of one church, so all of these things were new to me. My wife and I found a church within walking distance of our apartment. I had only seen pews in movies and had never actually sat in one, let alone knew how uncomfortable they were for long periods of time, but I was told that if they made them too comfortable, people would fall asleep, and I guess in some services that is true.

The pastor of this church was a wonderful man who truly loved God. My wife and I and his family became very close friends. I still didn't dare tell my new wife or my pastor that God had given me the ability to see into the supernatural realm, and in this church the movement of God was very minimal. The pastor, in a spiritual sense, had his hands tied as to what he could do or say from the pulpit by way of the congregation as well as the deacons. But privately he and I would talk, and he felt that I had an incredible sense of what was going on with him as well as the congregation, spiritually speaking. My wife and I spent a lot of time with our new pastor and his family, and we had many good friends inside the church, but I could tell there was a sort of division among this congregation. It was a little like that old saying of the golden rule—if you have the gold, you make the rules—and I was beginning to understand that the people who were the largest contributors to the church had a lot to say about the sermons as well as the music and all other aspects of this church. The pastor at this church was just a part-time hired employee, and the real owners of the building and the land were the people in the church who had the most money; they made sure that everyone knew exactly who they were.

I have many reasons why I've always chosen to sit in the back of most churches, but I think this early experience as to where I was comfortable sitting may have come from this first church that my wife and I attended. In particular where you sat was basically your status in the church. We sat with all the common people in the back, and that was where all our friends sat as well, so we felt right at home. My pastor friend would ask me on occasion what my feelings were toward some of the deacons and elders. I felt as if some of them actually did know God, but I'm pretty sure none of them actually had a relationship. But if that's the way they were raised, then that's what they knew. I wasn't allowed in the meetings unless they were open to the congregation, but I could tell that my pastor friend's position in the church wasn't always appreciated. I didn't know until later that this particular church had gone through many pastors, and that was a little strange to me. The church that I had come to know the Lord in had been under the same leadership and pastor since the church first started, so the whole notion that pastors would get hired and fired did not make much sense to me.

One of the other things I didn't understand at the time was that at the church where I had accepted the Lord as my Savior when I was just a teenager, there were large angels outside the front doors. They would greet people by touching them on the head as they walked through the double doors. When you walked into the foyer of the church, there were angels among the people just walking around and even gathered together in some areas. In the main sanctuary, I would see almost as many angelic beings as there were people. Some were seated in what looked like spiritual balconies placed around the main sanctuary as well as others that would hover above the congregation. The presence of God was undeniable. But this church that my wife and I were attending felt much different—not because it wasn't as big as my first church, but because there was the lack of the presence of God. People sometimes have alternative reasons for being in church, like they were there to just check in and be seen. I couldn't always see demonic entities, but I could usually sense their presence. There were no large angels standing at the doors welcoming people in. Sometimes at the front of the church, there would be an angel here or there, but usually there were not at all. There was a church angel that was only on the stage when my pastor friend would start speaking, and only for a period of time, and then even that angelic being would leave. There was definitely no spiritual balcony around the main sanctuary, and the angels that were there were very few.

I have to admit that some Sundays were better than other Sundays, but with that being said, some Sundays were a lot worse. I had been in churches overseas that felt spiritually sterile, like there was no presence either way. All I knew was that staying quiet among this type of congregation was imperative. I had no question that they would have some type of an opinion of me and my gift, and I was pretty sure that that opinion would not be favorable. As usual my best option was to keep taking mental notes to myself but speak to no one.

Family

Within months after we started going to the church, my wife found out that she was pregnant with our first child. I was very excited about this because I was older than my wife and wanted to start a family as soon as possible. Because of my job while I was in the military, I really didn't think I would ever have kids; truthfully, I didn't think I would live long enough to do so, but in Christ Jesus, all things are possible. I was also very excited about being a dad; of course, in my mind I wanted to be the best dad ever. I wanted to make every effort possible to be involved with my kids and help them as much as I could in any way I could, from start to finish. I wanted to do things the right way.

I think it's only natural that you would want to be better to your kids than your parents were to you, and in my case I felt that my early childhood was good, but it went downhill fast, and I wasn't going to allow that to happen to my marriage as well as my kids. Along with everything else a newly married couple has to deal with, my wife and I kept piling more on our plate. I guess when you're young, you don't think about all those things. Looking back, we may have bitten off more than we could chew for the early part of our marriage. By the end of our first year, not only were we going to be to parents, but we would also be first-time homeowners, and in my family that wasn't something that had happened very often.

As I mentioned earlier, my wife's family was very close in comparison to my family. They had all grown up with Christian beliefs, and church was not an option on Sunday morning. Her mom was an incredible individual who loved God with every ounce of her heart. She was tough when she had to be, but she was kind and gentle to everyone that she came in contact with. My wife's mom and dad are the very definition of "salt of the earth," and I don't believe they ever turned away anyone from their dinner table or their prayers as well. My wife had an upbringing that in many ways I was envious of. Her parents had always lived in the same house and still live there to this day. They never chose the easy path of divorce, even though marriage wasn't always easy, and they trusted God to see them through the tough times. I didn't have much in common with them, but I knew they were always going to be my role models as to how my marriage should go. I don't know if my wife appreciated what she had as much as I did, but I felt that we had the rest of our lives to emulate what her mom and dad had achieved.

That first year flew by, and by winter my wife had given birth to our first beautiful baby girl, with blond hair and blue eyes just like her daddy had when he was young. My wife's military career was going great. We had lots of friends whom we had met through our church and the military, we had our very own house and paid rent to no one, but the cherry on top was our wonderful baby girl. My wife and I had begun something that I had never thought was going to be possible—a family of my own—and I was so proud. I didn't even care that my job was at the nursing home where I had to change adult-size diapers. Inside I had a smile from ear to ear, and even though the church that we were attending hadn't lived up to what the angel had told me while I was in Germany, at least I was going to church. When the angel had spoken to me, I had felt as if I would have been given instructions, some type of direction to take me to a new place in my walk with God and maybe even a chance to use this gift I had been given. Patience had not always been my strong point, but in this case, I had no choice but to wait for God to open that door in my life. I knew he was preparing me for something; I just didn't know what.

I would soon find out that I was truly built for this whole Mr. Mom thing. I loved being a husband, and I truly embraced being a dad—and that meant every aspect of it, from bathing to dressing to changing diapers. I really did love every part of it. We even changed my work schedule so that we didn't have to take our daughter to any day care except for when we went to church services. Being a husband and a dad up to this point was one of the greatest things I had ever achieved in my entire life. The world has a saying that all good things must come to an end; well, in my mind my life was about as close to a bowl of cherries as it could be, and for me things were only going to get better.

Chapter 9: Storms on the Horizon

My stepdad, who was a loadmaster in the military, was called upon to fly supply runs in Desert Shield. I was never given any information as to what had happened, but I was told that my stepdad had suddenly become very sick, and my mom asked me if I would come out to the West Coast and help her take care of things. So my wife, our new eight-month-old daughter, and I drove out to the West Coast. At this point in our life, we couldn't afford to fly, so driving was the only option, and the car we had was the old Pontiac station wagon. We obviously weren't going out there to impress anybody, and the best we did was probably about twelve miles to the gallon, but we made it without a lot of problems.

When we arrived at my mom's house, we were informed that it was much worse than we anticipated, and instead of coming out to help my mom take care of things, it turned out that we were saying goodbye to my stepfather. I'm sure that people didn't see him the way that I saw him; yes, he did have an alcohol problem, and yes, he probably smoked far too many cigarettes. But to me at that time in my life, he was like an angel sent from heaven. Before I knew him, I had been homeless for quite some time until my high school friend's family decided to let me stay with them, but my stepdad found out and was outraged and insisted that I live with him and my mom. He not only supplied me with a wonderful home and probably the best food I had ever eaten in my life, but he also quietly showed me things like how to manage money and how to fix cars and houses. He never really told me he loved me unless he was heavily under the influence of alcohol, but in a thousand other ways, I knew he loved me. He never told me he was proud of me, but in my heart, I knew he was. Knowing my stepdad was a turning point in my life to put me on a path to be the man that I am now. Without him I'm not sure what my outcome would have been, and I am eternally grateful for this man being put in my life.

Going to the hospital with my mom and holding her hand was one of the hardest things I had ever done up to this point. My stepdad had meant more to me than my own parents. God had prepared me spiritually, but in the natural my stepdad was put in my life to show me a new path, a better path. When I saw him, he had lost so much weight, and his voice was even quieter than usual. He and I talked in whispers, and just for insurance for his and my peace of mind, as well as my mom's, we reviewed John 3:16. This was also the man who had first told me about tithing, and he was the epitome of the right hand not knowing what the left hand is doing. He tithed in absolute secret. Not even my mom knew he tithed to one of the local churches, but when he and I went on drives together, he would take me with him to the church and explain to me what it was that he was doing. He would say, "I don't think your mom would understand."

It was at this time in my life that I came to understand who the angel was standing at the foot of his bed. This angelic being stood there smiling, waiting patiently for my stepdad to say goodbye and escort him to his new heavenly home. I know that other family members were present as well, but thinking back, the only people that I can remember are my stepdad holding my mom's hand and the angel at the foot of his bed. I assured my mom that he was going to a wonderful place and that they would be together again someday for all eternity.

When I was in the military, on some occasions, I would see this same angelic being. Now working in the nursing home, I saw it as well, and I knew who it was, but with my stepdad it became so real, so permanent. I knew that my mom was going to be financially taken care of by way of the military and also things that my stepdad had put into place, but I worried about my mom spiritually and mentally as far as how she would handle losing my stepdad. This was not going to be easy for her or me, but it would be harder for my stepdad's son and daughter, who were also very close to me. I know that they were not related to me by blood, but at least in my mind, they were as close to me as any sister or brother, and my heart and prayers went out to them as well.

Within days after we arrived to help my mom, my stepdad passed away. My wife and I were put into the awkward situation of helping my stepbrother and stepsister pick out a casket as well as other funeral arrangements, but it took some of the burden off my mom and allowed her to start this grieving process. At the funeral among all the people, I noticed a small number of angelic beings off in the distance, but the majority mingling among the people were dark spirits. All I cared about was my mom's well-being, and I am sure that I should have probably cast out all the demonic presences, if only for a while, but I didn't. I just stayed quiet and held my mom and my wife as closely as I could.

Many people came to pay their respects, both friends and family as well as military members. For my family it was kind of a reunion, and I believed it helped my mother to get her mind off everything that was taking place. At the reception things went more or less back to normal. They had food, alcohol, and cigarettes, but for the majority of the people who were attending, this was how you dealt with these types of situations; it was the only way they knew. My wife and I stayed as long as we needed to make sure my mom was OK, and other than staying in phone contact once we returned home, there was not a lot we could do from halfway across the United States. We would have to depend on one of my sisters who lived in the area as well as my stepbrother.

Dealing with Pain and Trusting God

Within months after returning home from my stepdad's funeral, my wife found out that she had TDY orders (temporary duty). We had a few months to prepare for this assignment, but it meant that I was going to be a single parent for about three months. I would also be the first time that my wife would be away from me as well as our one-year-old daughter. I had the help of our church friends, as well as the military and my pastor friend and his family, but this was all going to be new to my wife. All I knew to do was pray and try to keep in as much contact with her as possible. Obviously, I could not call her, but she was able to call me as much as she could. At this point in time, cell phone technology was fairly new, so keeping in contact with each other was not easy. As always, the date for her to leave came way too fast, and the next thing I knew, she was on a plane leaving, and my daughter and I were going home to our house alone. I had stopped working at the nursing home because I didn't want to put my daughter into day care, and it didn't make any sense for me to pay almost as much for someone to watch my daughter as I was making, so my wife and I decided that I would start working again after she got back from her TDY.

Everything was going as well as it could. My pastor friend and his family would watch my daughter at least once a week. She knew them well, and it would give me a day during the week that I could go and do errands by myself. But even on the days they would watch her, I would try to get back as fast as possible, for right now she was all I had, and I did not like being away. My wife and I talked on the phone as much as we could, and all the phone calls felt as if our relationship was as strong as it could have possibly been under the circumstances. I would have flashes from time to time about my first wife calling me when I was in tech school in the military, and in a single phone call, it went from, "I love you" to "Your annulment papers are on the way; please sign them and send them back." I knew that it was just a demonic influence trying to put thoughts in my mind, but when you're by yourself you have way too much time to think, and in the pit of my stomach, I was concerned.

In the spirit I was rather confused, like I was having a spiritual tug-of-war with myself. The first month my wife was gone, we would talk about anything for as long as we could. Sometimes we would talk about what she did that day, about people that she had met and friends that she was making while on her TDY. I would tell her about all the wonderful things that our baby girl had done that day, as if she were the most accomplished baby on the planet. There were always people whose names kept coming up because they were people she directly worked with. As always, there were both good and bad things going on throughout her day, but she had one particular friend whom she talked about more than the rest. Due to the fact that there are about one hundred guys for each female, this new friend was a guy. She would assure me that they were just friends and that he was married and had a wife as well; he was there on a TDY assignment also. Spiritually speaking, I wanted to believe that what had happened to me before in my first marriage was just an isolated incident. The part that over the next few months started feeling familiar was the fact that the phone calls became less frequent, and the calls that we did have were very short. I didn't really voice my concerns to my pastor friend because I wanted to believe with every ounce of my heart that this couldn't happen to me again. I prayed to God that these feelings I was having were all in my head and that in reality my wife would be home after the three-month period and everything would be wonderful again. But the closer we got to the three-month mark, things started to change. She told me that she needed time to think about what she wanted to do, that things had changed. All I knew was that I wanted my wife back and that my baby girl needed her mom. But even well-meaning Christians sometimes allow Satan to confuse us. He will try to take you down a path that you never had any intentions of traveling but somehow, here you were.

I didn't want to believe for a minute that things were spiraling out of control. I had felt this way when I was a kid and my stepmom kicked me out of the house, and then she and my dad moved back to the Midwest and left me. My mom was not in a good place in her life and couldn't allow me to live with her; as a result, I became homeless. My first marriage ended in an annulment after a short period of time while I was in the military because during the time I was away, she found someone else. And now in my second marriage, I was in trouble again, only this time, I had a one-year-old daughter and a wife who was trying to figure out whether or not she wanted to come back to us. She said she needed time, but her new friend was with her, and my daughter and I were a long way away. I knew things weren't always perfect between us, but I didn't think that there was anything that most other newly married couples didn't deal with. I would pray every moment that I was able to. The only person that I had to talk to was my pastor friend, and he kept asking me what it was that I wanted to happen. Each and every time, I would say all I want is my family back, just me, my wife, and my baby girl.

My wife told me that they were going to keep her on the TDY a few weeks longer than they had first said. That wasn't unusual in the military because they have to find someone to replace the person who's leaving, and sometimes that person shows up late. But in this case, while my daughter was taking a nap, an angel appeared to me, kneeling down in front of me as I prayed, and told me that my wife had gone to be with this new friend. And if that wasn't enough, it also told me that my mom was going to need my help soon and that I would have to go to her. Over the last three months, I hadn't talked to my mom much because I was dealing with a lot of problems that I didn't really want her to know about.

That evening I received a phone call from a woman who said that her husband was going to divorce her because of my wife, and that they had both left their TDY assignment and were staying together in Florida planning their future. She asked me if my wife had said anything to me about a divorce, and I told her that all my wife had said was that she was considering it. Then she proceeded to ask me if it was OK if she came out to meet me so that she could in some way get back at her husband. I discouraged her and said that I thought that would be a bad idea because in truth I wasn't ready to give up on my wife not coming back to me. Regardless of what it looked like, God was still in control. She told me that I was being foolish and that my wife and her husband had been together almost the entire time they were on their TDY and that it had only continued once they got back to Florida, so in her opinion, I was believing for nothing.

Standing in Faith

The next day I received a phone call from a doctor in California telling me that my mom was not doing very well and that he felt that she should be admitted into a nursing home or some kind of care facility. I told him that my sister and stepbrother lived out in California and that they should be able to take care of her. He said that this was not the case and she needed some type of home health care. He asked me if I could come out to California and assess the problem and see how we wanted to proceed. I reminded him that I was in New Mexico, and even if I wanted to get out there, it would take me a few days. He said that he understood and gave me his number and told me to get back in touch with him when I had made the decision. I knew that an angel had come to me and told me that my mom was having problems, but I didn't know the problems were going to be this serious.

I talked to my pastor friend, and all he could really say was to pray about it and give it to God.

The truth was he was exactly right, but in a crisis like this, it really wasn't what I wanted to hear. So once again, while my daughter was sleeping, I came to God in prayer, and once again, an angel appeared kneeling down in front of me and said, "You have done everything for your wife that you can humanly do. Go, take care of your mother, and trust the Lord with your wife's well-being. Gather up yourself and your daughter, and know that the Lord's hand is with you."

The next day I talked to my pastor and told him what I was supposed to do. He asked, "Do you still believe that your wife is going to come back to you because you have every right to divorce her due to her unfaithfulness in your marriage."

I answered, "In my life I haven't always been perfect—far from it—and the word says that I will be forgiven as I forgive, so I will do my best to do just that, and the rest is in God's hands."

With that we packed up our old car, just my daughter and me. We prayed over our trip and that the vehicle we were driving would make it safely. My daughter really didn't care what it was we were doing, just as long as we were doing it together. By this time, I was her whole world, and she was the most perfect child on the planet as long as her daddy was in sight. We didn't have air-conditioning or cruise control, but we did have God and each other, and for now that was all either one of us needed.

I had let my wife know that we were leaving to go to California to help my mom get back on her feet, as the angel had told me, and I had done everything I could to convince her. Now it was between her and God. I will tell you that when you're driving halfway across the country with a fifteen-month-old child and an AM/FM radio that only gets reception near the larger cities; you have a lot of time to think and pray. Demons of deception would try to tell me everything was about to go wrong in my life; they would once again try their best to play that little movie inside my mind and convince me that I had to buy a ticket to the show that they wanted me to see. I couldn't see the angels that were traveling with me and my daughter, but I could feel their presence, and I knew that things were happening. Most importantly I knew that God was dealing with my wife and on a different level. I felt that whatever situation I was going to face when I reached my mom's house in California, I would somehow be able to handle it and still change diapers on the side. Last but not least, I prayed that this old bucket of bolts that I was driving would somehow perform another miracle and make it all the way there and all the way back.

Arriving at my mom's house always felt familiar to me. This was the house that I had only lived in for a few years while I was in high school, but it was the one house that felt like home. When my daughter and I arrived, we were to go straight to the hospital where my mom was. For the most part, they were just trying to get her prescriptions squared away because she had gotten off track and was having problems. When I got to her, she was complaining that they didn't really need to call me all the way out to California that she was just fine and could take care of everything once she got home from the hospital. The doctor and the nursing staff said that she was doing considerably better from when she came in. I was thankful that at the hospital, the familiar angel was not at the foot of my mom's bed, and hearing her complain about why she was there in the first place was a good sign to me.

It wasn't long before she was able to come home. Because my daughter and I had no real place to go, we decided to just make a mini-vacation out of this; I would maybe even take my daughter to her first amusement park. Within a few days after my mom returned home from the hospital, I received a phone call from my wife. It was kind of like the phone call I had gotten from her when she told me she needed time to figure out what she wanted to do, but this time she said she wanted to come out to California because she was really missing me and our daughter and she wanted to come out to help us with my mom. Now, inside I wanted to yell at the top of my lungs, "Glory to God in the highest."

But what I said was, "You can come out here, but know that when you do, we will be in separate rooms."

She agreed, and we continued to talk for quite some time. I hadn't told my mom anything that had been going on between me and my wife. She had been a military wife as well, and she knew that my wife was on a TDY assignment and never questioned why she wasn't with my daughter and me. When I told her that we were going to the airport to pick her up, my mom didn't ask anything at all. But what she did question was why we didn't sleep in the same room; we did our best not to let her know. But soon my mom grew tired of the company and was hinting to us that we could return home anytime we wanted. My wife had taken leave after coming back from her TDY, and things were going as well as possible between us, so we decided to take a trip back to the Midwest to see my wife's parents and family. Besides that, it gave us a lot of time to talk things out between us and figure out a few adjustments we needed to make in our relationship. All I knew was that God was faithful in restoring my family back to me. I also knew that we had a lot of work to do together to keep this from happening again, but I think it was something we both wanted, and for now that was enough.

When we arrived at my wife's parents' house in the Midwest, they were aware of some of the things that had taken place, so I was pretty sure that my wife was going to receive more than her fair share of counseling sessions with her mom. We stayed in the same room, but that was about it. I think that between us, we made the excuse that our daughter was staying with us in the room, but in my mind, there was a little more to it than that. There was always a sense of peace and calm at my in-laws' house; I knew that in the beginning, they didn't approve of me much because I was quite a bit older than their youngest daughter. But they did their best to try not to show it and made me feel like I was part of the family, even though most of the time I felt like a puzzle piece that didn't quite fit in. They were farmers and cattlemen, and I was a kid from the city and really didn't know much about tractors, combines, and other types of farming equipment. But I was pretty good at sitting quietly and acting like I knew what they were talking about, even though I am almost positive that they knew I didn't.

Church Split

In the spirit there was always a quiet gentleness, a sense that God's presence was always here, and by the time we left my in-laws' house, my wife and I were doing considerably better. I guess hours and hours in a car with no air-conditioning and only an AM/FM radio must have been the perfect situation for us to talk about our relationship and our life. Once we returned home, even though it felt like we were tiptoeing around each other, life was getting back to normal. My wife went back to work on base, and I started a new civilian job on base as well. Luckily, people in our church didn't know anything had gone on between my wife and me except for my pastor friend, and he was very good at keeping things to himself. But soon things in the church felt very different to me, almost like sitting under an air-conditioning vent and not knowing where the cold air was coming from. When we would go to church, I began to observe groups of people talking among themselves and even more demonic entities huddled in and around them as well. The group of people whom my wife and I were friends with were younger couples in the church who had small children and the deacons and elders always stayed within their small groups and insisted on sitting in what they felt were the places of honor during church services. Heaven forbid if anybody sat in those seats because they were going to get an earful. All of the regular attendees knew where not to sit, but the unfortunate people who would on occasion come to visit our church would almost have to be warned on where to sit and where not to sit.

On some occasions, I talked to my pastor friend and told him that I didn't know what was going on with some of the deacons and elders, but I had a bad feeling about it. He told me that they did not approve of some of the messages that he had been preaching and that if he continued to preach unapproved messages, he would find himself out of a job. Now I didn't know much about how churches and church business worked, but I had never heard of anything like this. To me you are a man of God preaching God's word straight from the Bible, but it turns out that some people didn't want the whole Bible taught, just the pieces that they liked, I guess. My pastor friend felt like he was walking on eggshells around his own church. Even though we were good friends in and outside of the church, I had never opened up to him and let him know that I was given the gift of sight in the spirit. I felt as if it might change our relationship if I said anything because I was unable at this point to even reveal this to my own wife, let alone my pastor whose job was hanging on by a thread.

In the weeks following, the church elders and deacons called a meeting that most of the regular attendees showed up to. My wife was very familiar with church splits, but I on the other hand had never heard of such a thing. At this all-church meeting, my pastor friend was not allowed to talk, only the deacons and elders, who explained why they were firing our pastor and that one of deacons was going to stand in until they hired the replacement pastor. Apparently, they did not like the fact that he was bringing in some new music that wasn't found in our hymnals as well as a multitude of other topics that they did not agree with, so he was on his way out. Most of the younger couples continued to meet with him and his family until they were able to get another position preaching in a different church a couple of states away. My wife and I didn't have any family close by, so for us our church was our family, and now due to this church split, our spiritual family was going in a multitude of directions. This was not what we needed at this time in our life, but it did push us to seek out other churches and find a new church home.

By this time, our daughter was a little more than two years old, and the church we were leaving behind was the only church family she knew. One afternoon my wife and I decided to take my daughter to a fast-food restaurant near the church; it had a nice inside play area. It wasn't often in public places God would allow me to see into the supernatural realm, and sometimes I questioned why this was so, because I know there are both light and dark spirits in these public places. At this particular restaurant, when my wife, our daughter, and I sat down to eat our food, I realized that there were dark entities present in the room—not just ones that I could sense, but I was being allowed to see them in the spirit. My wife commented about why I was so preoccupied with the people around us in the room, and I replied, "No real reason; just things feel different today." As I watched my daughter play in the play area with the other kids, I did my best to not look obvious that I was staring at other people while they were eating and watching these entities interact with them. At one point a dark spirit started moving around our young daughter and would from time to time look back at me with a crooked grin. As always I would cast these entities out in Jesus's name, and they would move away out of my field of vision, but not so far that I could not sense their presence. At one point I was even shown a short vision of my daughter lying lifeless on the ground. Not quite knowing how to handle this flash vision that appeared in my mind, I decided it was time for our family to go home. As my wife and I finished our meal, because my daughter was too interested in playing with the other kids to finish her meal, we informed her that it was time to go home. She did the best a two-year-old could do to argue the point; we stayed a few more minutes, and then we were on our way out the door and into the parking lot. What I had noticed was this dark spirit from a distance followed my daughter, but not so close that I thought it was following her. My wife had gone on ahead and was going to open up the car and start the air-conditioning when our daughter, who was already at this time a little strong-willed, decided that she was going to run and catch up to her mother in the parking lot. As she ran this random dark entity seemed to get closer and closer. I wasn't sure what the intention was, but instead of casting it out in Jesus's name as I should have done, I started to move a little faster to get to my daughter. By nature I am very protective, and as per my military training, I become a bit overprotective of my family, friends, and loved ones. By the time I reached my daughter, a car had started to back out of its parking space on the side of the restaurant. My daughter, being short, was not seen by the driver of the car, and when the car started to move backward, I rushed behind the vehicle and pushed my daughter forward toward my wife just as the car ran into me. The car wasn't very tall, and my legs were pinned underneath the rear axle. The license plate luckily folded up like tinfoil once it came in contact with my shoulder. The witnesses claimed that I purposely ran behind the car so that it would hit me. The manager of the restaurant came out to see what was happening and called the police. The driver of the vehicle was a young teenager; her friend was a passenger. They told my wife that they were supposed to be somewhere and left the scene.

I don't know what the witnesses were thinking. Perhaps they thought I was trying to extort money from either the driver of the car or the restaurant, but in truth I was just trying to save my two-year-old daughter, and the only one who could back up my claim was my wife. The police officer asked us if we wanted an ambulance, and we declined but went on to the military base hospital to get my shoulder and leg checked out. As the dust settled, I could see the demonic entity that had been following my daughter as if he had won some minor victory, but all I knew was my daughter was safe, and all I had was a few minor cuts and bruises. Other than that no actual harm was done. In retrospect I should have continued to bind the demon and not receive the vision I was given, but some lessons are learned more slowly than others, and this lesson I would not soon forget.

God has given us authority and dominion over our thoughts and visions, in Jesus's name through his sacrifice on the cross. He wants us to pray over, speak out, bind, and have confidence that God is a good and loving Father and wants the best for his children. Luke 10:19 (NLT) states, "Look, I have given you authority over all the power of the enemy, and you can walk among snakes and scorpions and crush them. Nothing will injure you."

Chapter 10: A Time to Speak

I had heard about a church in town that was more like the church that I had become accustomed to when I was a teenager living in California. The church that my wife and I had just left was not the type of church I was used to. There was nothing wrong with singing out of hymnals if that's what you are used to, but for me, I had no idea in the world how to do it, and my wife was constantly trying to help me, to no avail. This new church had a projector, so you would just sing the words off the wall; I could do that. I suppose this church was quite a shock to my wife, but in many ways, I felt right at home, so we came to an agreement when we first started attending this church that we wouldn't actually sit down in the church until praise and worship stopped. My wife really enjoyed hearing the senior pastor speak; in her words, it was like he was speaking directly to her and no one else. We only sat in the balcony where my wife felt safe and where we could come and go from the service and not interrupt anyone or really even be noticed. For me it was fun, like a Southern Baptist church; people would yell things like "Hallelujah!" and "Praise the Lord!" for no reason. Sometimes they would even dance in the aisles or bang on tambourines. I have to admit, it was a little distracting, but the message that the pastor would teach was always incredible. My wife felt the pastor at this church was like nothing she had ever heard before, and even though the congregation was a little bit crazy, his messages were always worth the craziness. For me in the supernatural, it was more like a dinner and a show. Yes, there were the occasional demonic spirits lingering about, usually outside here and there, but they were so far outnumbered by the angelic entities that it was almost not worth mentioning. I had to really focus to get a bearing on the actual congregation, because what I had come to realize was that half of what I was seeing were actually angels. There were angels moving among the congregation, there were angels seated in the balconies, and there were also angels on the platform with this pastor while he spoke the word of God. There was so much angelic activity that I hardly noticed the occasional outburst from people in the congregation or even the tambourine lady (who was really hard not to notice). I think for the first time in quite a while, my wife and I felt like we were actually hearing someone speak about the word of God and how it applied directly to our lives, and for the first time in quite a while, the angels would actually speak to me. I would see them in different places throughout the congregation or on the platform where the pastor was. Most of the time, they didn't acknowledge me or the fact that I could see them, but on occasion they would talk to me from a distance, and it was like they were standing right next to me. For the first time in a long time, I heard the word *seer*. I knew that this was their way of acknowledging the fact that they knew I had a gift, and suddenly in this new church, even though I still wasn't allowed to say a word to anyone, there were entities in this church that knew what I was able to do.

After a few months had gone by, we started to get to know some of the people in the church and even getting to the church in time to hear praise and worship music. I had talked to the pastor on a couple of occasions but really just to introduce my wife and myself. We had already had one pastor friend who had been forced to leave and go to a different church in a different state, and until I learned more about this church, I wasn't going to allow myself to get too close, even though there were angelic beings telling me that this was a safe place and that this particular pastor would listen to what I had to say.

One evening during a special service, my wife and I were sitting in the balcony as always. There was the usual angelic presence throughout the sanctuary, but one particular angel to the right of the stage from where I was sitting kept motioning to me so much that my eyes were more fixed on the angel that on the pastor or what he was teaching. As I watched this presence that had manifested to me in the spirit, I started hearing words being said like this angelic being was standing right next to me, but in fact I was seeing it on the stage rather far away from me and my wife. The angel was pointing at one of the ushers and said, "Seer, tell him that you can see the angels on the platform. He will know what to do."

My first thought was that this probably wasn't a great idea. We knew this particular usher because he was prior military, and he was very outgoing and talkative—someone you can't help but like.

The angel repeated to me again, "Seer, tell him that you can see the angels on the platform. He will know what to do."

My wife nudged me and said, "What's wrong? You're squirming a lot."

I said, "I think I'm going to go down and say something to that usher to the right of the stage."

She asked, "Why would you do that?"

I answered her with, "I really don't know, but I think I'm supposed to."

And with that I got up went downstairs and walked down the right-hand side of the church sanctuary where this particular usher was standing.

The service was almost over, and when I approached the usher, I said, "This is going to sound strange, but there are quite a few angels in the sanctuary, and one in particular that is on the stage told me to tell you that I could see them."

I think I may have added, "If you could keep this to yourself, I would appreciate it," but his response was, "I will tell the pastor after service. I think he would want to know this."

I took a deep breath, sighed, and thought, *Well, here we go; they're going to try to cast demons out of me.*

I went back to my seat with my wife, and she asked, "What that was about?" I told her that it was nothing really; just something I felt I needed to do.

I really wanted to leave the service as fast as possible, and usually my wife was in agreement, but for some reason on this particular evening, she wanted to talk to some people. I'm not an overly tall man at six feet, but I am muscular for my height, so it is a little difficult to hide sometimes in a crowd. The next thing I knew, the usher whom I had spoken to came to me and asked if I could go talk to the pastor. He said he had some questions for me. My wife was in the middle of a conversation, but she did overhear what the usher had said and gave me a rather strange look.

I told her, "I'll be back in a minute."

The usher and I walked up to the front of the sanctuary, where the pastor was talking to other members of the congregation.

As soon as he was free, he looked at me and said, "You can see angels."

I answered and said, "Sometimes, yes."

He said, "Tell me what they look like. I want to know everything about them."

On this subject I was a man of very few words; it wasn't like I had been able to talk about it at length to anybody on the planet at this point in my life.

The next words I said were, "Please don't tell anyone that I have told you this; even my wife doesn't know that I am able to see into the supernatural realm. This has always been my secret, but the angel that was standing over by the usher told me that I was to tell him and he would know what to do. I guess he was supposed to tell you."

The pastor said that he understood that I didn't want anybody knowing about this gift, but he went on to say that he had a seer in the church years earlier and that he felt having a seer in the church was very beneficial. He went on to tell me that whenever I was comfortable with it, he would appreciate me letting him know what was going on in the church, spiritually speaking. We both looked at the usher, who was standing close by, and asked him if he could keep the secret.

He said, "Of course, but can you let me in on the things you are seeing in the spirit?"

The pastor looked at me and said, "Is that OK?"

I answered and said, "I suppose that would be fine."

But what I was really thinking was that I had no choice because these two people were now aware that I was making the claim that I possessed this particular spiritual gift. Not knowing exactly what they were thinking behind closed doors, I would have to just trust that this information would not become church gossip, and then I would have to explain to my wife why we were looking for a new church. What hadn't dawned on me was that the angel had given me these directions to tell this particular usher. I just had to trust that God would not allow me to reveal this information to somebody who would spread it around.

Church went like this for several months. I would give the pastor or this particular usher small insights of what I was seeing the spirit. I didn't dare share with them the entire picture of what I was seeing because I wanted to walk this out in small steps. Due to the pastor and I having these conversations fairly often, we began to spend time together and realized we had quite a few shared interests beyond church. He had been a high school quarterback and was well known for his athletic ability in the community, and his dad was a respected former coach at the local high school.

One Sunday evening, as my wife and I now had our favorite seats up in the balcony, I was observing people coming to the front of the sanctuary for prayer. There was one particular woman on the left-hand side of the platform who would cough every now and then. In the natural it didn't look like anything important, but among the other people who were receiving prayer for different things, she was off to one side by herself, and I noticed a dark entity that was moving about her legs and winding its way up close to her neck, and then she would cough. I told my wife that I was going to go down and speak to my usher friend. I told him what I was seeing in the spirit. So calmly and quietly, he went to the pastor and waited for him to finish praying for the person he was with and then he leaned in and gestured toward the woman I had told him about. My pastor looked at me and motioned that he and I would pray for this particular woman together. As we prayed, she fell to the ground and started shaking violently. One of the demons that I had seen with her left almost immediately, but the second dark spirit was doing its best to not let go. As my pastor and I cast out the evil spirit in Jesus's name, it pulled away, but not so far that I couldn't see it, then it rushed in quickly and came right up to my face, so close that I could almost feel the pressure of the word it spoke—"*Seer*"—in a disgusted voice. Then he proceeded to move away beyond my field of vision. The woman looked like she was asleep on the floor down at the altar, and I know some people were a little alarmed, but she looked so peaceful lying there. My usher friend and I stayed with her as the pastor went on and prayed for other people, and within minutes she sat up and began talking. When I felt everything had calmed down, I went back to my seat up in the balcony next to my wife and sat down.

She looked at me and asked, "What was that about?"

I smiled a little bit and said, "Something inside me told me that the pastor was going to need a little assistance praying with her, so I was just being obedient."

Youth Group

The associate pastor at the church was also the youth pastor. This was another incredible man of God. Wanting to serve in the church, I decided to work with him upstairs in the youth group. This was sometimes a little crazy, but it was controlled chaos, and there were often a good number of demonic entities to deal with and cast out. The majority of the demonic entities I had to deal with were those of deception as well as demons that would function in a sexual manner. Often, I would pray with the same kids week in and week out about the same things, doing my best to try to educate them that they had as much dominion over these entities as I did. For some reason it was hard to make them understand that the entities weren't leaving them because of the words I said, that the power was not in me as a person; it was in the name of Jesus that we as Christians were to have dominion over all the darkness of the earth.

What I didn't let the kids in the youth group know was that often, I could see on them what they were dealing with in the spiritual realm. In some ways I'm sure this was cheating, but it was God who had given me this advantage. At this point in time, I didn't tell the youth-group pastor that I had this spiritual gift. I knew that he and the senior pastor were very good friends, and I was unsure if it had been talked about. I just did what I felt I was being spiritually led to do in a very quiet fashion, and if the youth pastor was aware, I don't believe he ever mentioned it to me. But I really enjoyed working with the kids; it was always exciting, and the youth pastor made it fun. In his own way, he was a big kid as well, playing all the games with them and never allowing them to win anything if he could help it. On the rare occasion that he would actually lose any of the contests that were held, the kids would always make sure that he was well aware of his loss, but because the youth pastor was himself was very competitive, that didn't happen very often.

Men's Advance

Within the first few months that we had started going to this church, they had a men's conference up in the mountains. Because I was new at the church and didn't really know what it was about, I chose not to attend the conference. But this year, I felt much more comfortable with the church and the pastors, and it was a wonderful event. I told my wife that for three days, I was going to go with some of the men from the church to this campground that they had gone to the year before. There weren't very many men who went up, maybe a few dozen or so, and in the spirit, there was a lot of activity among the men. It was the closest that I had ever been in my life to being able to speak freely about what it was that I was seeing; I think most of them assumed that my wife knew that I could see in the spirit.

At this conference I was able to talk to some of the men and give them words that the spirit was giving to me. I felt that after all these years, this silent spiritual gift that I had been given actually had a purpose. No one at this event looked at me like I was crazy; they would only ask questions and want to know details about what it was I was seeing in the supernatural realm. The men would sometimes huddle around to listen to what I was describing, and it allowed them to feel, in a whole new way, that they were closer to God. They would even make the comments and say that they wished they had this particular gift, and in my mind I thought, *If you only knew what you are saying, you wouldn't ask for it*, because in my life, it meant silence—silence to the point of almost breaking under the weight. Being a seer to me meant an extremely heavy burden to cart.

When I returned home, I thought that my wife would be asking a series of questions, but that never happened. I believe that God understood that my wife was not quite ready to hear about my spiritual gifts. I was very aware that in most church settings, my type of spiritual gifts were not only not welcome, but were viewed as if I were in some way demonically possessed, so at this point in time, I was still very careful to only open the door and allow people access as to what it was I was seeing in the spirit. I love my wife very much, but we had just been through a major speed bump in our marriage, and at this point in time, I wasn't willing to test things out to see if she was willing to accept what I had been hiding all this time.

Some months later, after coming back from the church's men's conference, my wife and I found out we were pregnant with our second child. Our walk with God was improving week by week, so we were both very excited about the new arrival to our family. Our daughter, who was now three years old, was also excited that she was going to become a big sister. Only being a few months pregnant, my wife and I received word that my mother's health had begun to decline once again. The hospital called me and explained that she had been taken to the hospital due to mishandling of her medications and dehydration as well as the continuing deterioration of her vital organs. I asked the doctors if they had been in touch with my sister or my stepbrother. They said they were having trouble getting in touch with them, so they had moved down the list to me. We decided that my wife would put in for emergency leave from her job in the military and we would go out as a family to California and find out what the best options were for my mother's health and well-being.

Once again, we packed up the car and drove the two-day trip to the West Coast, where I was born and raised. When we reached the hospital where my mom was, we first talked to the doctors and were warned by them that she had lost a considerable amount of weight. My mom had always been very athletic; she was a long-distance swimmer and had stayed active for many years. When my wife, my daughter, and I went into the room and saw my mother for the first time in almost a year, we were at a loss for words. She had dropped around fifty pounds. She looked so frail to me, like she may break when I gave her a hug. She insisted that she was fine to go home by herself and that she was more than capable of doing things on her own. I was just relieved that when I walked into her room, there wasn't an angel at the foot of her bed waiting to take her home. My hope was that we could possibly get her back to health and allow her to be independent once again; she was only sixty years old but looked much older. But the doctors insisted that she would need constant supervision and care, either by a family member, nursing home, or a type of home health care. My wife and I discussed the situation at great length and had made a decision that she would come back to New Mexico and live with us at our house. We also realized that our house was probably not big enough for the new baby who was to come in a few months as well as my mother, so we decided that once we returned home, we would put in for military housing and see if we could get into a bigger unit. It was also decided that my stepbrother would live in his dad and my mom's house, which would make moving my mother to New Mexico much easier because we had agreed to leave all the furnishings and just take personal items on the trip back home. He had been renting an apartment, and this looked like a good solution that would help him out as well. After all it was his dad's house and the house that he had grown up in. We had also decided that we would bring my mom back in her motor home, which would be more comfortable for everyone. My mother was still rather defiant that she would be just fine living in her own home, but with the help of the doctors, we persuaded her that this was the best idea. She had made it clear that she was not going to a nursing home at sixty years old, so this was the best option for everyone. It was decided that my wife, who was pregnant, would drive our car packed full of her belongings, and I was to drive the motor home packed with as much as we could carry, as well as my mom and our daughter. It was an interesting trip home.

Our timing was very good as far as my wife and me getting into base housing. They had just built a new housing addition for the military, and my wife was smart enough to get us on the list early. The house that my wife and I had bought was very crowded for the four of us, and soon we would be bringing in a new member of the family, making space even tighter. Within a few months, we had been given clearance to move into the new base-housing units. It was a four-bedroom duplex with two bathrooms, and it was perfect for the four of us, soon to be five. We didn't really want to sell our first house, so we rented it to a young couple that we knew, and it worked out well because the renters were paying our bills on the house, and we were able to put back a little bit of money on the side for possible repairs.

My mother had not been to a church service in her life that I knew of, but if you were going to live at our house, you were going to go to church on Sunday morning. At first my mother wasn't really sure about this idea, but later it became the highlight of her week, and it was also a guarantee that she was going to get out of the house and be around lots of people who enjoyed her company. She was in a wheelchair, and our church was in a very old building that did not have wheelchair accessibility, so one of my friends from the church who happened to be very tall and strong would help me carry my mom up the steps to the main sanctuary in her wheelchair.

She wasn't sure about the music so much in the church, but she absolutely loved to hear our pastor speak the word of God, and to her, it was as if he were speaking directly to her. During her life she had only heard about religion and different denominations, but this was the first time that she had ever heard that she could have a personal relationship with God, and it was as if she couldn't hear enough. When we went home, she would insist that instead of putting music in the cassette player in her bedroom, we would play an audio series of the Bible so that she could hear the word of God the entire day. When we would finish at the book of Revelation, we would just go back to Genesis and start the whole Bible from the first book again.

Soon she came to the decision that she needed to give her life to God, but she wanted our pastor to do the salvation prayer with her. Within only a few months of living with my wife and me, my mom gave her heart to the Lord and decided that she was going to spend the rest of her days getting to know God better.

Even though her mental health had improved, her physical body continued to show signs of wear and tear from earlier in her life, decisions that had been made and maintained for decades of her life. Food was her biggest struggle; nothing ever sounded good, and more often than not, when she ate, it didn't settle well in her stomach. The ministering angels that I would see with her at church and sometimes at home were with her more and more. Everything in her was at peace, which was evident to us, but sometimes it was hard for her to articulate her thoughts. Before we knew it, my wife had given birth to our second child, another beautiful baby girl, and my daughter, now three and half years old, was thrilled to be a big sister. My mother couldn't have been happier because she had hoped that she would be with us long enough to get to know and help with our new arrival. My mother continued to get weaker and weaker, and the doctors had told us there wasn't much that they could do to help her, that her heart, her liver, and other organs were in very bad shape, and had she not moved back with my wife and me, she would have surely passed away much earlier. But we were going to enjoy the time we had, and we thanked God for extending her life and giving us this extra time.

Going Home

Within a few short months after our second daughter was born, the ministering angels that had been with my mom were replaced with an angel that was familiar to me. I did not know this angel's name; I just knew that this particular angel was here to take my mom home. Her passing wasn't immediate, but it as if they were preparing her for the journey; my mom had lived with us for almost one year.

That specific day has always stayed very clear in my mind. My oldest daughter and I were playing in the living room, and my younger daughter was asleep in the same room where we were playing. There was a long hallway, and at the end of the hallway was my mother's room. In the final weeks of my mother's life, she developed a slight rattling sound as she breathed, and other than my daughter and I playing as quietly as we could, trying not to wake the baby, we could hear in the background my mom breathing. As we played the house became silent, and even though my oldest daughter was very young, we looked at each other, and somehow, she and I both knew that it was way too quiet. I told her to stay there and continue playing and that I was going to check and see whether Grandma was OK. When I walked into the hallway and looked down toward my mother's room, I saw the ministering spirits. They had not talked to me very often, but when they did, it was always significant.

The ministering spirits said, "Seer, your mother is no longer here. She has gone to be with the Father." And that was all that was said.

Not that I didn't believe what was spoken to me wasn't true, but I walked the length of the hallway and walked past the ministering angel that was posted at her door. I could hear the cassette player in her room still quietly speaking the word of God, our holy Bible. She looked like she was sleeping, resting quietly. I reached down and checked her pulse. Not feeling anything, I rechecked the pulse in her neck. Still nothing. Lowering myself to my knees, I grabbed my mom's hand. It was cold, but that was not unusual, and I started to pray, thanking my Lord for the past year that I had been blessed with. I felt like I'd been given the time to get to know my mother in a way I had never known her in my childhood or as a young adult. I had been given extra time, so I could allow her to go and not have any doubt in my mind that not only did she know God, but also that she had professed him as her Lord and Savior.

I felt at peace. The next thing I knew, there was a small hand on the back of my head, and my oldest daughter asked, "Did Grandma go to be with Jesus?"

I replied, "Yes, she did, and she is with him now."

She asked me, "If she is with Jesus, then why are you crying?"

I said, "Because Daddy is selfish, and I won't get to see Grandma again until I go to be with Jesus in heaven."

She then bent down onto her knees like her dad and grabbed a handful of my shirt and just stayed there with me. At that moment in time, my sweet little girl was so much stronger than I was, and somehow, she knew that I needed her strength, so she stayed. After a little bit of time passed, I got up and picked up my daughter, and we went back into the living room, where the baby was still asleep. The ministering spirits that I had seen at the door followed my daughter and me down the hallway and into the living room. I called my wife and told her that my mom had passed away.

Because we lived in base housing, the military authorities had to be notified. Within minutes, the military police as well as an ambulance came to my door. When I turned after letting them in, I looked at my daughter still playing on the floor as the little one remained asleep at the other end of the living room. The ministering angel had knelt down on the floor next to my oldest daughter as if to comfort her. They loaded my mom onto a stretcher completely covered by a sheet and put her in the back of the ambulance. The military police stayed and asked questions; afterward, they told me I would have to go to the base hospital to identify my mother as soon as they were done taking the report. Before they were finished, my wife had come home so that she could comfort me as well as stay with the kids while I went to the hospital to finish the paperwork. When I looked back into the living room where my oldest daughter was playing on the floor, the ministering angel was no longer there. Maybe it was just that I couldn't see them any longer, but as always, I wasn't in control of what I saw and when I saw them.

Kissing my wife goodbye, I basically followed the military policeman out the front door and proceeded to get into my car and drive to the base hospital. My wife and I lived in base housing, but it was not on the military base itself. It was located right across the highway, so it was about a ten-minute drive to get to where I was going. As I drove down the street from my house, I made a right turn. Then, coming to a stop sign across from a convenience store, I had to make another right turn;

as I made the second turn, everything inside my car went completely white. My eyes searched for something, but all I could see was a woman's face. She had dark hair, and if I were to guess, she looked to be about thirty years old.

Her voice sounded familiar, and she kept saying, "Look how beautiful this is. Look at the ocean. It looks incredible." And again she said, "Look how beautiful this is; it's just like you said."

Then I realized it was my mother that I was seeing! She was much younger, younger than I ever remember seeing her, and she was describing things that she was looking at as if I could see them as well, but all I could see was her. She continued to describe things to me, and I tried to communicate to her that I could not see what she was describing, that she was in a different place, not where I was. But she kept on describing as if not understand the words that I was saying. Then I heard a tapping, and at first, I didn't know where it was coming from.

Turning to my left, I saw I was at the gate of the military base, and the gate guard was asking me, "Are you on your way to the hospital? They're expecting you; do you need help getting to the hospital?"

I said, "No, I know where it is. I'm so sorry; I'm a little bit out of it right now."

He said, "I understand, and I am so sorry for your loss."

I told him, "Thank you."

Somehow God had allowed me to see a vision of my mother and allowed her to describe what it was that she was seeing in heaven in those first moments of her being there. I felt so much peace; I was so thankful. As I arrived at the hospital and went in, they were all waiting for me, and like the gate guard, they all told me how sorry they were for my loss and said if there was anything they could do, to let them know. I looked at my mother one last time and then was asked to sign some documents. It was all over very quickly, and before I knew it, I was back home with my wife and two girls, trying to figure out what was going to happen next. We had decided once the autopsy was done that my mother should be buried next to my stepdad in California, and we made the arrangements to have her sent out before us. The military gave my wife emergency leave status, and we were able to pack up the girls and leave for California soon afterward.

No Time to Mourn

My stepbrother had been living in the house in California for the last year that my mom stayed with my wife and me in New Mexico. When we pulled up to the house, I told my wife that something felt strange. As we walked to the front door and rang the doorbell, no one answered, but because it was my mom's house, we still had a key. We proceeded to open the door, and when we did my strange feeling became instant reality. My stepbrother must have had several cats in the house, and by the strong smell, I doubt they had a litter box to use. Almost all of the furniture was gone. The house was so strong with the smell of cat urine that my wife and I were afraid to take our two girls into the house, and when my stepbrother came home, I felt as if he had a little explaining to do. He told me that his girlfriend had moved in with her cats and that they had been running short on cash and decided to sell most of the furnishings that were in the house so they would have money to pay the bills. Now my stepbrother was a college professor, and I knew that he made pretty good money, and I also knew that he'd had financial troubles in the past. But living rent free in my mother's house for the last year, I just wanted to know were all my mother's things were; the only answer he could give me was that they were gone. Not only did the house reek of cat urine, but the demonic entities that had been present through much of my childhood and young adult life had taken up residence in my mother's house as well, which would explain why my stepbrother was in the position he was in both financially as well as with his female houseguest. It was obvious to my wife and I that his new girlfriend had conned him out of almost everything in the house, either for her own gain or for her own personal use.

My stepbrother was far more intelligent than I was, and in the academic realm that made him my superior, but when it came to size and strength as well as the ability to handle myself in hand-to-hand confrontation, I outranked him by quite a bit. When the conversation went from my stepbrother trying to outdebate me to a physical confrontation, I found myself in a very comfortable situation. As I held him against the wall with one hand while his feet dangled six inches off the ground, I made my point clear that after the funeral and my mom was laid to rest, he was to leave the house and my wife and I would be left to clean up his mess. I then proceeded to cast out demonic entities, including my stepbrother and his guest, because they had no place in my mother's house. After I had completed the spiritual housekeeping, my wife and I had to begin the physical cleaning that had been neglected for quite some time.

We then began the process of all the preparations of my mother's funeral. Because of the condition of the house, we had to do enough to make it livable, so we started with having the carpet removed and the concrete floor scrubbed and sealed. After that, we focused on the task at hand, giving us no time, up to this point, to mourn the loss of my mother.

As family members began showing up, we did everything we could to make them as comfortable as possible. Due to the condition of my mother's house, we didn't have much furniture so we did the best we could with what we had. I had no question that my mom was in a good place, but the ability to see into the spirit reopened my eyes to the fact that the majority of my family members still needed to be properly introduced to the Lord Jesus. Being the little brother gave me few occasions to speak into my family's life. Prayer has always been one of my spiritual strong points, so I took this opportunity to make sure that in every situation that called for prayer, I was going to take the advantage of whatever I was given.

Everything during the funeral went as well as it could under the circumstances. After the dust had settled, my wife and I got busy putting my mom's house back together, as well as taking care of my mother's final wishes as to how she wanted things dispersed in her will. We had decided to sell the house. Unfortunately, the entire renovation budget was going to come out of our pocket with the belief that we would be reimbursed at the sale of the house. It took a few weeks to get all the necessary repairs finished and up to code, but before we knew it, we had completed the task and had a realtor in place so that we would be able to go back home where we were stationed in New Mexico.

Peeking into Old Doors

A few months after returning home from California, my wife was told that she would be attending a leadership school so that she would be able to be promoted to the rank of noncommissioned officer status. This was a mandatory school that everyone in the military had to go through. It was kind of like her going on a TDY assignment but in this case, she would not be leaving the town that we lived in or the base where we were stationed. One condition of the school was that she had to live on base for the duration of the school. We were both OK with this because on most of the weekends, the girls and I would be able to visit her. In the beginning when we would talk or visit, everything was going very well, but soon, like the changing of the weather, I started sensing in the spirit that things were changing—things that were familiar to me from the past that I had hoped were behind us. The group that she was with at the school began hanging out after school and doing more and more activities together that didn't include a husband and kids. I knew this feeling. The sensing that I had was far too familiar; it was a road I had been down and really didn't want to travel this way again, especially now with two kids. Once we open these dark spiritual doors in our lives, these entities often come back to revisit, to see if those doors in our lives are actually closed shut or if we are willing to open them up once again. Sometimes we are just deceived in the fact that we think we are strong enough to handle things on our own.

In the leadership school on base, there were predominantly single military members with an occasional married and divorced person sprinkled in. When they weren't in school or studying, they enjoyed hanging out and partying whenever possible. Even though I wasn't really the partying type, there was one weekend that they were going to get together, and my wife invited me. It was then that my gift of seeing in the spirit allowed me to see things for what they really were, and the presence of the spirit of deception was everywhere. All I could think about was how fast I could get out of this environment. My wife asked me if we could please stay. I suppose by this time in our marriage, I should have let her know that I could see things in the spirit, and this particular party was crawling with far too many dark spirits for me to want to stay. I knew that things were happening in the dorms on base that went a little beyond studying for the pending graduation, but I had no actual way of telling her I knew, and even if I did tell her, would she think I was crazy? I just wasn't willing to risk my marriage.

So, as always, I prayed and asked God for a window of opportunity to be able to ease into this conversation about what had been going on while she was in leadership school. I needed to know if our marriage was still important to her or if this group of new friends had changed her mind. My wife and I had gotten married shortly after she had gotten out of technical school for the military, and I had always felt that part of her wanted to experience what it was like to be a carefree college student, a rite of passage. I knew that part of her life had been bypassed. Marrying me and starting a family meant that she would have to grow up and be a serious adult possibly before she was ready. But as we all know with anything that's worth fighting for, there are going to be high points and low points; this was just another learning experience for both of us. It did expose some weak spots in our marriage that at some point we were going to have to address and improve.

Meeting Face to Face

Shortly after my wife graduated from training school, our church was holding another men's conference up in the mountains of New Mexico. It was a great time to get away from the day-to-day life and focus on God as well as growing closer in our relationship with him. Since I had joined the church, this was my second men's event up on the mountain. The first advance that I had been to was life changing for me because I was able to flow without putting a lot of thought in what people would think about me. I still held most of what I was seeing in the supernatural to myself, but what I was able to give had been received and appreciated.

There were several churches from New Mexico represented as well as Texas, probably close to a hundred and fifty men or more. A group of us traveled together in one of the church vans along with our pastor, and the hours on the road gave us quite a bit of time to get to know one another in a one-on-one setting; if nothing else, the trips were always entertaining. Once we arrived at the campground and were assigned our cabins, we would generally settle in and acquaint ourselves with our roommates. We were all there for the same reasons, and that was to get closer to God and try to improve as men and husbands as well as brothers in Christ.

On the first evening, service went the way it had gone the year before, singing and praising God as well as listening to a pastor speak from one of the several churches that were represented, and it was always a wonderful message. For me it was like being a commentator at a football game; my pastor would ask me what I was seeing in the spirit, and I would do my best with my limited vocabulary to explain to him what I was seeing. Many times I felt inadequate because the words I was using to explain what I was seeing could not really begin to describe the angelic presence, but this was only my second time being allowed to flow in this type of setting, and I still held back most of what I saw because it sounded far too incredible.

On the Friday night of this event, the spirit of God was so powerful in this large room. I was up in the altar singing a worship song with about seventy-five other men when an angel appeared in front of me and said, "The man that is standing behind you is in need of your forgiveness."

The angel was rather large, much larger than some of the ministering spirits that I was used to seeing. In my mind, I thought this should not be a problem because it had always been easy for me to forgive people for most anything in my life. God had blessed me with a rather short memory when it came to people who had wronged me. I knew that if I wanted to be forgiven of my own shortcomings, then I needed to be forgiving of my fellow man. So this would be a piece of cake. I went to turn around to see to who I was to extend this forgiveness. The angel in front of me stopped me and said, "This is the man that your wife had intended to leave you for, the man that tried to convince her that she needed to divorce you so she could be with him. It's up to you to turn and forgive him or not; it is your choice, but like most choices in our life, this one will not be an easy one."

Turning back toward the angel that was in front of me, I asked myself if I could do this. Everything inside of me wanted to turn and break this man into a thousand pieces, and all of me had to hold back what I was trained to do in the military. I had a choice to turn and be a lion or to allow the gentleness of God overtake me and be the lamb that he wanted me to be. I would love to say about myself that this was an easy decision, but that would be a lie. I had made many hard decisions in my life to this point, and I wanted to show the love of God. On that day on the mountain, I had to die a little bit to myself and allow God to consume a piece of me so that I would be capable of this act of forgiveness. Keeping in mind I was not a small man, I turned around, and I had no idea of what to expect of this other person. As I faced this gentleman standing behind me, he was much smaller than me and was crying so hard that mucus was running down his face. Our eyes met. I could see the entity of fear with him; it overtook him so much that he momentarily passed out, falling to his hands and knees. I quietly said, "In Jesus's name, I bind you, spirit of fear, and cast you out." God is so good because instead of turning and feeling anger, I felt sorry for him. I knelt down on one knee and I said, "I forgive you, my friend."

He looked up at me and said, "You have no idea in the world what I've done to you."

I said, "I know exactly who you are and what you've done. God has revealed these things to me. I don't know what kind of miracle it took to get you and me here on the same mountaintop, but for God all things are possible, and all I know is that I have been asked to forgive you."

He asked me, "How can you forgive me so easily?"

I said, "Do you think this is easy? As a man I know how I would like to handle the situation, but Jesus says that if I am to be forgiven, then I need to forgive, and I am not a perfect person. I ask for grace every day of my life, and it is because of this that I can say in Jesus's name that I forgive you."

He had been on his knees, and it was at that moment that he stood up and put his arms around me and hugged me. He said, "I don't know if I would've been able to do that."

I replied, "Don't say too much because I might start thinking about other options."

Still shaking, he laughed a little, and after the service was over, we sat and talked for about the next three hours. He mentioned that he had wanted to approach me the first night; because we all had name tags with our first names, he knew exactly who I was. He said that he had no idea that I was that big and that he even thought about leaving the mountain in fear that I would physically injure him.

The guys whom he had come up with convinced him to stay and approach me. They said, "We don't know what we're going to do against him, but we will back you up the best we can."

The next day after the morning service was over, the group that I had ridden up with in the van piled back in and started sharing on the trip home about things that God had done while we were up on the mountain. By nature, I am rather quiet, so I just sat and listened to what God had been doing in all these men's lives.

But my pastor decided to ask me a question that I had heard so many times: "Would you share with us what you saw upon the mountain in the spirit?"

I began to tell them what had happened, how through the grace of God I was able to extend forgiveness to one of my brothers in Christ. After telling the story, God's presence was so powerful in the van that we began to cry so hard we had to pull the van over so that we could regroup and continue the trip home.

When the church van arrived at my house to drop me off, I went to the house to see my four-year-old daughter as well as my six-month-old daughter and my wife standing in the kitchen with her back to me. She turned and said, "How was the mountain?"

I was not sure how to answer her because I knew that she hadn't heard from this individual whom I had met on the mountain for over a year. I decided to tell her the truth, but the response that I got from her was not the same response that I had received in the van on the way home. I wasn't personally responsible for the encounter; I'm pretty sure that was God, but either way she wasn't very happy about it. Almost immediately I could see a dark entity come alongside of her, so quietly under my breath, I bound it and told it to leave in Jesus's name. I knew how this worked, and I knew that the dark entity would probably come back to put a multitude of thoughts into her mind. We had come home from the mountain on a Saturday, and for the rest of the day, other than my two little ones, it was rather quiet in our house. Sometimes quiet is better.

Casting out the Past

On the following Sunday morning at church, I was pretty sure that she felt exposed even though it was really only a couple of pastors from the church and a good friend of mine who were in the van with us on the way home who knew anything. But because Satan is a liar, I'm sure that she felt the entire church knew our business. Maybe it was because of what happened while she was at the leadership school on base, or maybe it was because she had put this person from her past far behind her, but whatever it was, she was struggling. After service, our pastor asked if everything was OK. I said that I had told her what it happened upon the mountain at the men's advance and that I thought it had opened some old wounds. He suggested we come back that night and sit down in his office to discuss some things and see if we could work through any problems that we were having. My wife felt pretty safe with our pastor and his wife, so we agreed to come back that Sunday night to try and talk through some of the things that were causing us to struggle.

Sometimes keeping things to myself causes me problems, and this was one of those times because my wife was still unaware that I had the gift of sight into the spiritual realm as a seer. Some of the men in the church knew that I had been given this gift, and I'm sure they were under the impression that my wife knew. My pastor, on the other hand, was completely aware of the fact that I wasn't comfortable with her knowing this about me. I know it was probably wrong of me, but I felt like we had other mountains and our marriage to overcome, and I didn't need to add any question marks as to my sanity to make things worse. When we came to his office that evening, our pastor's wife took our four-year-old to the kids' part of the church, where her children had already been playing. Our six-month-old was asleep in the carrier, and we decided to put her in the back of the pastor's office in case she woke up. We began the meeting with a short prayer and began to talk about different issues, some matters that I had been dealing with as well as concerns my wife was feeling. Suddenly my six-month-old daughter started to cry, and I have a bit of a motherly side to me, so I went back and picked her up, changed her diaper, and gave her a small bottle of milk. I had stepped outside of our pastor's office, but the door was still open, and I could hear our pastor and my wife still talking. As I finished with our daughter, I walked back into the office where they were sitting, and I could see in the spirit that there were several spirits of darkness that had appeared in the room. The pastor was in the process of telling my wife details about her past, things that I did not know that could have only been given to him by way of the spirit. He had told her many things that only she knew, things about her childhood, and she began to cry and ask God for help.

My pastor looked at me almost in amazement, and I said, "What just happened?"

He asked me, "What do you see in the room right now?"

I told him that there were several dark spirits, and he told me to lay my hands on my wife and start casting them out. I said to him, "They're not really in her; they're just in the room."

He said, "Cast them out anyway."

When I told them leave in Jesus's name, all but one left the room almost immediately. The one that stayed lingered off to one side in the corner of the room and just looked at me. In my pastor's office, there were four eight-foot-tall windows in the room. As I started to say, "In Jesus's name..." the windows started to shake like they were coming out of the windowpanes. This dark spirit came across the room and moved a large wingback chair, slamming it up against a wall. My wife was still sitting in her chair with tears running down her face, and my pastor looked at me in bewilderment. I was at of a loss for words because I had never seen this type of manifestation. Before I knew it, the dark entity came back across the room and struck me on my side, knocking me into my pastor's desk.

With that I said, "In Jesus's name I bind you and cast you out, and you are not to return again in Jesus's name!"

After that, the room went quiet. My wife grabbed a Kleenex and was wiping the tears from her cheeks. My pastor with a slight smile said, "I've never seen that before."

I looked at him and lifted up my shirt, exposing my rib cage and the bruises that had been left by this dark spirit. He asked me, "Did that spirit do that to you?"

I said. "I guess so."

I am not even sure that my wife knew what was going on in the spirit or in the natural in my pastor's office that night. I wasn't even sure exactly what had taken place, but I know that my wife changed. It was the most incredible change that I'd ever seen a person in a short period of time. I believe without a doubt she was a new person after that encounter, with a new love for God and a newfound relationship with the Lord Jesus. I'm not sure if it was at that moment that my wife realized that I had been given a gift, and we never really talked about it, but from that moment on, our life changed, our marriage changed, and I know that God had performed miracles not just in my wife but in me as well.

Chapter 11: Youth Groups and TDYs

Due to God's anointing as well as the success of an incredible youth-group leader, the youth group in our church continued to grow larger and larger—so large that we had to move from the upstairs of our church down the street to a one-hundred-year-old abandoned theater. Having youth-group services in an old, abandoned theater sounds very cool, but this old theater had been used for many different things over its lifetime. As I have found in other old buildings, some dark spirits don't leave easily just because the people cease to frequent these uninhabited structures. On the one day a week that we would have our youth service, a small team of people would go in before the church service started and pray over the building. The entity that we were constantly dealing with was a spirit of deception that often manifested itself as fear. The boys in the group always tried to put on a brave face, but many of the girls liked to stay in groups because in their minds there was safety in numbers. At times some of the kids thought the building was cool and spooky. For me it often felt like we were trying to herd chickens into a building, but once we got the kids in the building and they were focused, we knew that our youth pastor would always have an incredible word to speak to the kids as well as the youth leaders.

Before my wife and I knew it, the military had put my wife in for another TDY assignment. Our oldest daughter at this time was over four years old, and our baby girl was thirteen months. My wife assured me that this assignment was going to go well and that she would try to call and talk to me in the girls every day if she was able to. Taking care of the girls and church took up a large portion of my time, and up to this point in time, my wife going on TDY had not been good for our family. But we were confident that this assignment was going to be different. This time we were going to trust God and allow him to walk things out in our lives, and we were going to be victorious in our time apart from each other.

While my wife was still overseas during the month of July, my two beautiful girls and I decided that we were going to watch fireworks in the small town where we were stationed. We decided to go to a parking lot across from the high school where we could set up lawn chairs and watch the Fourth of July show. My oldest daughter who was now four was an old pro at this, but to my youngest, who was only about fourteen months old, this was all new, and I was curious as to how she would respond to the fireworks. We found a parking spot and proceeded to put out our lawn chairs; other cars were also pulling into the parking lot to watch the show. After we had been there for about thirty minutes, a car pulled in with their music turned up extremely loud. The volume of the music wasn't really the problem; what was the problem was the explicit language that was being used as lyrics in this individual's choice in music.

By this time most of the parking lots had filled up, and finding a new spot would have been difficult. I couldn't really see the people who were playing the music because they were three or four cars away, so carrying my little one and holding the hand of my four-year-old, we walked down to ask the people playing the loud music if they could please turn the music down because I didn't want my little kids hearing that type of language. There were a lot of things happening in the spirit, and most of it was not due to the presence of angelic beings. The spirit of fear by this time was present on most of the people who were in the parking lot with us. Sensing the dark spirit that was present around these people, I began to pray under my breath for a Psalms 91 hedge protection to be placed around myself and my kids as well as the people in the parking lot. As I approached the car, a man in his late twenties stepped out of the car and walked up and stood in front of me. Still holding my young daughter in my arm, with my four-year-old daughter still holding my hand, I asked him if he could please turn the music down because I really didn't want my daughters to hear that type of language. The man just stared at me, and almost as if this demonic spirit peered at me from behind one side of this man's head, under my breath, I started to say a prayer. The man said, "I don't know what you're mumbling under your breath, but if you and all these people don't like my music, you can just leave."

With that he pulled a .45-caliber handgun out from behind his back and put the barrel of the gun about five inches from my forehead. My two little girls had no idea what was going on, but it was clear to me that the people parked in the parking lot with me knew exactly what was going on because everyone started getting in their cars, starting their engines, and squealing out of the parking lot. The only thing that was going through my mind was that if I hadn't had my two girls with me, I could've easily disarmed this young man, but with both hands occupied, I was very limited as to what I could do.

I said to the man, "I am going to turn around and walk back to my car, put my two little girls in their car seats, get in my car, and drive away."

He said, "If you turn around, I am going to unload this magazine in the back of your head."

I said again, "I'm going to turn around slowly walked back to my car and put my kids in their car seats."

He responded by saying, "Don't you dare turn your back on me."

Slowly I turned around and started to walk back to my car. I lowered my younger daughter down to my waist as low as I could carry her because I felt like if he was going to shoot me, it would be either in my head or my chest, and I didn't want any of the rounds, if they were to go through me, to possibly hit her. The Bible verse that kept going through my head was Isaiah 41:10: "Fear thou not for I am with you, be not dismayed for I am your God, I will strengthen you, I will uphold you with the right hand of my righteousness."

In the background behind me, I could hear a woman yelling at the man who was holding the gun. I wasn't listening to her words; I just wanted to get to the car and get my girls into their car seats. When I went around to the passenger side of the car to buckle them in, I didn't look up to see where the man was at; I just wanted to get out of there. After that I walked back around the front of the car, opened the driver's door, sat down, started the car, and proceeded to back up and leave the parking lot. By the time I put my car in reverse, we were only one of three cars left in the parking lot. Every other car had left, and not one person said or done anything to help us. This wasn't the first time in my life that someone had leveled a gun at me with the intentions of grave bodily harm, and in truth there had been times in my life that there were no threats made at all; they just pulled the trigger and fired. But this was the first time that I had two innocent children with me. It wasn't that I was in fear for my own life, but the thought did cross my mind that this could have been a defining moment in the life of my two little girls, if for no other reason I wasn't about to let the spirit of fear enter in because my two baby girls deserved to grow up knowing who their daddy was. The police to my knowledge never knew anything at all about the incident, but I guess on the Fourth of July, they were too busy to notice the problems that were going on in this parking lot one block from the fireworks display.

My four-year-old daughter asked, "Are we not going to watch fireworks?"

I said, "I guess not this year, maybe next year when Mommy's here."

As we drove back to base housing, I was praising God that nothing had happened. We were all going to live to see another day, and my wife was going to have a husband and two kids to come back to. I caught a glimpse of the woman who was yelling at the man that was holding the gun, and something inside of me said that she looked familiar, but I felt like it didn't really make any difference; I just wanted my two girls and I to get home safe.

The next day I went out to the mailbox to get the mail. We had one of those big mailboxes on base that would hold the mail for about twelve different houses, and to get your mail, you had to have a key. As I was getting our mail, a lady walked up to the mailbox with her key and said, “I want to apologize for my brother yesterday. He is from a large city in Texas, and he thought because you had the baby in front of you that you are using the child as a shield. He thought that you are carrying a weapon as well and were going to shoot him.”

I looked at her and said, “I was carrying my baby in one hand and with the other had the hand of my four-year-old daughter. Just where did he think I was concealing the gun?”

She said, “I don’t know. He was a little bit drunk as well, so there was no telling what he thought. You can call the military police, but he’s already left to go back home in fear that he would go to jail because of what happened.”

All I knew is that God is good and there was a Psalms 91 hedge of protection around me and my girls, as well as all the other people in the parking lot. I’m sure that many people were scared and probably had an unbelievable story to tell their friends and family, but no one got hurt—except for my four-year-old daughter, who was really looking forward to watching fireworks. Luckily, there were fireworks on TV, and as far as she was concerned, that was just fine.

For Better or Worse

Before long my wife's TDY was over, and she was on her way home. We had talked on the phone more than we ever have before while she was gone, and the kids were more than excited to see her. We had scheduled a trip to the Midwest to visit my wife's parents as well as my dad and stepmom. Visiting my wife's family was always fun for me, but time spent with my dad and stepmom was always bittersweet. It was on this trip that my wife informed me that God had spoken to her and told her that she was to have a third child. She wasn't really sure whether it would be a boy or girl, but she had no doubt in her mind that this was the will of God, and it was going to happen.

Now it wasn't every day that my wife would say, "God told me I'm supposed to do this." In fact, it was the first time she'd ever said that in our marriage to this point. Before we had talked about only having two kids, and we agreed that it didn't matter if they were boys or girls; we were only going to have two. For my wife to make this statement was big, and on this trip to the Midwest, God had even revealed to us the name of our child, regardless of whether it was going to be a boy or girl. Now as for me, Mr. Mom, I didn't know if it was going to be in nine months or in the years to come; all I knew for sure was that we were going to have a third child.

It was always a big debate for my wife and me if we wanted to start our trip to the Midwest at my dad's house and get that part of the trip over with, or go to my wife's parents' house and start the trip off on a good note. Anytime we went to my dad's house, there was always a question mark as to whether we would be allowed to stay in their house and how long my stepmom would let us stay. We decided to go to my dad's house first and end this trip at my wife's parents' house, going home on a good note.

As soon as we rang the doorbell and the door opened at my dad's house, a spirit of deception would almost immediately come upon us, but my dad always loved to see us and enjoyed his time with his granddaughters. My dad was the fun grandpa whom everyone wanted to be around; he was the type of person who would do anything in the world for you, and my baby girls loved every minute they were able to spend with him. My stepmother, on the other hand, was constantly surrounded by dark spirits. She had allowed unforgiveness toward my mother and a hatred toward any of my mother's children to eat her up inside with physical as well as mental pain. My dad and stepmother's house was split level, so when we would come to visit me, my wife and kids would stay downstairs to visit with my dad, and most of the time, my stepmom would try to keep her distance and either stay in her room or in the kitchen upstairs. For me it was painful to go upstairs with the ability to see into the supernatural realm and not be able to help her.

She wanted nothing to do with me even, when I extended myself and asked if there was anything I could help her with. Her response was, "You can leave me the hell alone and go away."

Under my breath I would cast out demons, and for the most part, they would look at me with a crooked grin and leave the room, reentering the room as soon as I walked away and reminding her just how much she hated me and my family. One time the tension was so high that while my dad was at the grocery store and my wife and kids were downstairs playing with some of the toys that were kept at my dad's house for the grandkids to play with, my stepmother came about halfway down the stairs and accused my children of stealing the toys that she had for her grandchildren. She used a barrage of profanity telling us to just get out of the house and go home—"Nobody wants you here." In the spirit I knew it wasn't her own words that were being spoken, but it was the words of the demons that she had allowed to put these thoughts in her mind. She was so convinced that these thoughts were her thoughts, but they were only lies from the devil. For my wife and I, there was only so much we were willing to expose our two little girls to, and unfortunately for my dad, he would come home and get an earful from my stepmother, telling him that he needed to inform his son and family that they were not welcome here anymore and they needed to go, now! My dad had made a decision long ago that right or wrong, he was going to make this marriage work, and so to keep as much peace in his household, he informed us that even though we were cutting our visit short, it was time for us to go. Needless to say, my wife had already made that decision and was packing up our things.

That was the way most of the visits to my dad's house went. The visits were always cut short, and my dad would stand there with tears in his eyes, telling me and my wife as well as his two granddaughters how sorry he was that things turned out the way they did. From the very beginning when I would talk to my wife about my stepmother, she always thought I was exaggerating the truth, but by this time in our marriage, she had realized that I did everything I could to make my stepmother sound far better than she actually was. My wife knew that it was very important for our kids to know my dad, their grandpa, but she also knew the price we were going to have to pay for this relationship, as well as for my kids to be shielded from the fact that my stepmom wished above all else that we would never darken their doorstep. This was a balancing act that my wife and I had to juggle each and every time we would come to visit my dad, but to me the trade-off was worth it; they would have a relationship with their grandpa, who truly loved them and worshipped the ground they walked on.

At my wife's parents' house, it was a totally different situation. God was always present in their house, and her dad was an extremely hardworking man who loved God. My wife's mom was such an incredible person and would do anything for anyone, and my two little girls absolutely loved being at their grandma and grandpa's house, with aunts, uncles, and cousins. There was always more food on the table than we could possibly eat at one setting, with toys and yards to play in, the same yards and bicycles that my wife had grown up with, as well as story after story to be told and laughed about. This house in the spirit felt like joy, peace, and love. It was the house of abundance in all good things; it was the way we enjoyed ending our trip before we went home, and for the most part, it would allow us to forget what we had experienced at my dad and stepmom's house. I was always thankful for my wife's parents and family, and it was a constant reminder to lift up my dad and stepmom in prayer that someday they would know the peace that was felt in my wife's parents' house. It wasn't like I was able to see a constant influx of angelic entities at my in-laws' house; it was more just the presence of love and light that was there. After leaving my dad and stepmom's house, it was like taking a deep breath of fresh air.

After returning home from our trip, my wife and I's relationship was on an incredible path. Our relationship with God was growing in leaps and bounds. We had many good friends who supported us from our church as well as being involved in many of the activities. I enjoyed working in the youth group with one of the best youth pastors ever released on the body of Christ. He was an anointed pastor with a passion for teenagers. As much as I wanted to be a spiritual leader in the youth group, because of my size, I was often delegated to be a makeshift bouncer for the kids who either didn't want to be part of the youth group but were forced to be there by their parents or the ones that just couldn't get along with the other kids. They were forced to sit in the back of the sanctuary or, in our case, in the back of the theater with me. I suppose because of my size people, just assumed that I was mean, but my unruly group of kids and I would often have conversations about a multitude of different subjects.

I had one such conversation with a young man who had been forced to sit with me so many times that he decided that regardless of whether he was told to or not, he was going to sit with me anyway. I inquired as to why he was always getting in trouble, and he joked and said that really it was because he just liked sitting with me. But on further questioning, he told me that he thought he got in trouble frequently because we lived in a small town and there wasn't very much to do other than get in trouble.

Trying to be funny, he said, "Why don't you build something so we could have things to do in this little town?"

When he said these words to me, I really didn't think much about it. The problem was that his words stayed with me, and from time to time, I felt like God was trying to tell me something, using this young man to give me a prophetic word.

Walking on Pillows

Before long, the men of our church were planning on going to a different location for our growing men's advance. It seems that anything God has his hands on prospers, and the men's event that we held every year was no exception. We had outgrown the old campground that we had used for several years, and this new facility gave us even more room to grow. By now many of the pastors were aware of my ability to see into the supernatural realm and would frequently ask me what it was I was seeing in the spirit, as well as different ways that the spirit of God was manifesting around them as they were speaking in front of the men at the events. I always enjoyed my role as spiritual commentator for most of the pastors, and I like to think that it was beneficial to them even though I felt inadequate most of the time trying to put words to what I was seeing in the spirit.

On one of the nights during the worship service, many of the men had moved up to this large altar in the front of the sanctuary, and they were worshipping God. Many of them were on their knees with their hands lifted in the air, and at some point during the service; the presence of God just started overtaking many of the men. I could see in the spirit hundreds of ministering angels coming to lay hands upon these men as they were seeking God, and at one point of the service, my pastor pointed at me and wanted me to come up to the front where he was standing, I guess to put words to what was happening during the service in the spirit. The problem was there were about one hundred men lying flat on the floor side by side, and there was really no way for me to reach where he was at up on the stage.

At that moment, a large angel appeared before me and said, "The man of God has asked you to come to him and share what it is you are seeing."

I thought, *OK, I understand this; I'm just trying to figure out a path to get there.* The angel spoke up and said, "Just walk as a crow flies straight to where he is at."

Well, I can do that, but at 230 pounds, a lot of people are not going to be happy about that. Again the angel said to me, "Walk as a crow flies to the man of God."

I thought, *Well, Peter walked on the water, so maybe God wants me to walk on these men in a straight line to my pastor.* And that's what I did. The funny thing was it felt like I was walking on pillows not people. I did just what the angel had told me to do, and I arrived to where my pastor was standing. What he was inquiring about was what exactly I was seeing in the spirit during that worship service, and like a commentator, I gave him all the details that I was able to. After the service was over, many of the men said that they saw me walking on top of them, and even some of the men whom I had walked on said that they didn't feel anything as I did so, almost as if I were walking on a cushion of air above them. And many of them, even to this day, say that I never laid a foot on them as I walked to the stage at the front of the sanctuary.

The next day when we were all in the dining facility eating breakfast, the men were talking about what had taken place the night before, and as they began to share their stories, some of the pieces started fitting together, and they realized what God had done in that evening service. For me, it wasn't like I was Peter and had the possibility to sink down into the water, but as much as it was a sign to the men who had witnessed it happening, I learned to trust God in a whole new way. I didn't know what it was, but I felt that God was taking me to a whole different level that I hadn't experienced before, and I was going to have to trust him more than I had ever trusted him in the past. Spiritual growth isn't always easy, but it is absolutely necessary.

Once the men's advance was over and all the men returned back to their homes and churches, many incredible things were shared, things that God had manifested in the men's lives. As for my wife and I, we found out that we were going to be having a new addition to our family in August. The name had already been given to my wife while we were traveling back from the Midwest visiting our parents, so that was one small hurdle that we didn't have to think about, whether it was a boy or girl. By this time, my mother's house in California had sold, and after everything was paid for concerning my mother's estate, hospital bills, and burial expenses, my wife and I decided that the money that we were going to receive from her will, we would probably invest in a multiunit home for rental income. We began the task of shopping for a property to purchase; for us shopping for properties was also a source of entertainment. As often as we could, we would look through the different magazines in our hometown for potential properties. But for some reason the words that the young man had spoken to me in the youth group were ringing in my ears.

He said, "If there was anything to do in this small town other than get in trouble, I would probably do it."

I asked God what exactly this meant, and in prayer the answer that I was given didn't really make sense to me at the time. My wife and I just wanted to use the money that we had received as a down payment on an investment property, but every time I would pray about this, I felt like I was never given peace about this decision.

I wanted to be obedient as to what God wanted me to do with this money he had blessed me with, and even though we had potentially found a property that we were interested in, we stalled the deal; my wife and I waited on God. I had hoped that if God's intentions were for my wife and me to build a business from the ground up, he would at least give me a business I was familiar with. I had spent most of my time, as well as met my wife, in a fitness center; maybe that was God's will. But one thing that I know about God: if he asks you to do something, it's probably going to be something you're not very good at in the first place. This way, the only way it will be successful is if you put your trust, faith, and prayers in him and allow him to manifest the miracles before you. That was exactly what he asked me to do, and now I had to explain to my wife why we were not going to buy this multiunit fourplex but instead to go shopping for a bare piece of land big enough to build an outdoor recreation facility. And I thought telling my wife that God had given me the ability to see into the supernatural realm was tough!

I told her that God had given me the idea by way of a young man in our youth group who said that he felt he would get in less trouble if there were something for him to do in our small town where we had been stationed. I am not really sure if she just trusted me that much or if God had spoken to her as well, but the next thing I knew, we had put the fourplex on the back burner and started shopping for land to build an outdoor recreation facility. I kept thinking to myself that a fitness center was far more within the realm of something I would enjoy owning and running; the type of facility we were looking at building was very expensive and required a large space. After running some of the numbers, we calculated that we were only going to be able to build our business one section at a time. The facility we were thinking about as a finished product was going to have go-karts, a batting cage, miniature golf, bumper boats, paintball, and a possible arcade facility. In a larger city, these types of attractions can bring in large amounts of money, but in a smaller town we were just putting our faith in God and allowing him to work a miracle. By this time, we had finally told the realtor that we were not going to be buying the fourplex and that my wife and I were aggressively looking for land to start building our business. We had only enough money to purchase the land, and we would have to secure a large loan to even start the project, but once we found the land and prayed over it, we decided to step out of the boat as Peter did and trust God. We purchased the land on a busy highway intersection in early spring.

A month later our pastor had invited a man whom he had met some time before to come to our church as a guest speaker. This particular speaker was well known for giving prophetic words with incredible accuracy. Of course he wasn't going to have enough time to give everybody in the church a prophetic word, but like everyone else in the church, my wife and I were hopeful. As the guest speaker finished his message, he walked off the platform down into the altar area at the front of the stage, and he would point at an individual, and God would give him a prophetic word for that person. The church would record the message on a cassette and give it to you so you could listen to it later on, but as he would speak, most of the people we knew could testify even as he was speaking of the accuracy of the words that he was giving. As he came to the area in the church where my wife and I were sitting, he stopped and looked at us and pointed at me; he asked me to stand up.

The speaker, being an average-size man, walked up to me and then turned to look to the congregation and said, "Oh, God, please let this be a good word." I suppose this was due to my size. He looked back at me, and he said, "You will be a blessing to kids; you will bless kid after kid after kid, and money will come to you and flow through you."

Then he wiped his brow as if to brush away the sweat and said, "Boy, I hope that's what he wanted to hear."

Later our pastor came to us and asked if we had any idea about the meaning of the word we were given, and that was when we told him about the business that God had put in our hearts to build and that just the month before we had purchased the land. We told him it was going to be a fun center where families and groups and kids could go make memories. Even if it only distracted them for a short period of time, maybe that was long enough to make a difference in their lives.

My wife and I received the prophetic word as confirmation from God that we were going in the right direction and had faith that God would not allow us to stumble and fall but be victorious in everything before us, teaching us to trust him and to love our fellow man. It was if the faith I had been asked to exercise at the men's event earlier in the year was playing out, and instead of stepping out in faith and walking over men lying in an altar, we were asked to step out in faith and trust God that he would not leave us nor forsake us in our new business venture.

A Son and Business Too

The month of August finally arrived, along with a new addition to our family: my wife had given birth to a baby boy. Our oldest daughter, who was already a professional at being a big sister, thought that this was wonderful; my baby girl was just happy that she wasn't the youngest or the smallest in our family anymore. God had once again performed a miracle in our family, and I believed that this was as big as our family was going to get. I have no doubt that if God put it on our heart to have more children, we would have been obedient, but as it turned out, three was enough. Between being in the military and building a new business, this was about all my wife and I would be able to handle. Before long we had put together a business plan to take to the bank and see if we could secure a loan for phase one of our new business, which was to include a perimeter fence around seven acres of land, two bathrooms, a ticket booth, and a maintenance/storage building for the go-karts—not to mention the go-kart track and guardrail system. Between making meals for the little ones as well as changing diapers on our bouncing baby boy, we were building phase one of our new business project. Most people told us that we were crazy, that there was no way we were going to make this business work, but all I knew is that God had given me a vision, something that could have only manifested through him. We were to build this business to be a blessing to kids, and my wife and I both understood that money was going to come to us and travel through us. We were to be a blessing to this small military town, and God was going to have to pour out financial blessings for us to keep this whole thing afloat.

The first thing that I was going to build was a large shed that we would use for a maintenance building as well as storing the go-karts. A local construction crew was to begin the dirt work for the go-kart track, but within the first few weeks of the project getting off the ground, somebody came in during the night and stole most of the materials that we were to use to build the maintenance building. I knew that dark spirits were going to come against us, but for some reason, I thought we would at least get out of the gate before anything was to manifest. There were some people who felt that what we were building was wonderful and that it would be very good for the town as well as the base to have this type of facility built. There were also people who thought my wife and I were destined to fail, even good and well-meaning Christian people in our church who thought it was a bad idea. One particular member of our church who was a known builder in our town said that he had heard rumors that someone else was going to build this same type of business, only they were going to be a franchise and would surely put my wife and me out of business. All I knew was that God had put this business on our hearts, and then a man whom we felt spoke the word of God prophetically confirmed the business that we were to build, and that was enough for me. The dirt work continued, but I changed gears and began building the perimeter fencing instead of the maintenance building first, because if I couldn't keep the building materials inside the fence line, then not much was going to get done.

One by one I started putting fence posts into the ground, and by this time it was winter. A friend of ours allowed us to borrow their travel trailer so that I could stay on site and keep thieves from stealing our supplies. I believe that God was teaching me to pray, because I had always prayed over my meals and a multitude of other things, but it was at this time that I began to understand what it was to pray without ceasing. Ministering angels would come to me and just walk with me; I would look at them, and they would respond with a faint smile. I would just nod my head to acknowledge their presence, and I would go about my work. When I first began to put the fence post in, I was using a handheld posthole digger. I know it sounds funny, but I have always been a very physical person, and digging post holes with a manual digger was just fun for me to do. But it wasn't time efficient, so we rented a small bobcat with an auger on the front, and in a short period of time, all the holes had been dug and were ready for the fence post and concrete. Sometimes friends from our church would come out and help me, usually on days that we were pouring concrete. I would feel energized when my friends from the church would show up. Most of them were willing to work just as hard as I did simply because they wanted to be a blessing to me as well as the body of Christ and the kingdom of God.

Once we got the posts set in concrete, as soon as possible, we would string up the chain link fence, first on the west side of the property, then on the north side of the property. On one evening as I was preparing for a concrete truck in the morning, snow started to fall, heavier and heavier until I couldn't even see the holes in the ground that we were preparing to pour on the next day. Most of the postholes were only a few feet deep, but the main poles were around four feet deep. In order for me to clear them out with my handheld posthole digger, I had to get on my knees, and the handles would just stick out of the hole enough for my hands to hold on to the end. Being tired, sore, and hungry—not to mention freezing cold—I had gotten down on my knees and was pulling debris and snow out of one of the holes. It was one of the deep holes that was much wider than the head of my handheld posthole digger; once I got to the bottom of the hole, I would just throw the digger in, and whatever handle was left sticking out was what I would use to pull the snow and debris up and out of the hole. Then I would repeat and drop the digger back in, go down to my knees, and repeat the process.

I remember my hands being extremely cold due to my gloves being wet from the snow. I threw the digger down for the last bit of debris at the bottom of the hole and just sat there with my hands sitting on the tip of the posthole digger and my forehead resting on top of my hands. It was past midnight, and I was tired, wet, and cold. I just sat there like that for three or four minutes. I may have been praying, but I don't really remember; something in me wanted to just give up and quit. Then I looked up from my gloves and saw the hem of a robe in front of me.

The ministering angel looking down at me said, "Noah looked just like that when he was building the ark, and he had thoughts of giving up as well. Be strong and don't give in; you are sowing into a harvest field."

I kept cleaning out the holes until the entire east fence line was finished. I had worked through the night, and just like clockwork, my friends showed up to help me, and the concrete truck came right on schedule. We were three-quarters of the way finished with the fence line. Once the south side fence and gates were installed, I was able to go back to work on the maintenance/go-kart storage building. Juggling the three little ones along with building our new business was a challenge. My oldest had started kindergarten, but on the days that we were pouring concrete, I would put my two little sidekicks in day care; on all the other days, they would stay with me at the construction site while my wife was at work. We had a large blue panel van that we had outfitted with padded carpet and a TV that the kids had nicknamed "the disco van" because of the multicolored lights in the ceiling. The van was big enough that we could eat meals together as well as take naps. When it was chilly, we could plug it into a 110 outlet to provide heat; all in all, we had a wonderful time, and we have some great memories involving the disco van. Meanwhile the construction crew that was building the go-kart track was moving along at a record pace, and once they had finished pouring all the concrete and pit area for the go-kart track, it was my turn to come in and install the guardrail system. By this time, it was spring, and the weather was getting much warmer; soon we would be opening the go-kart track to the public.

We had an assortment of people who had worked on the park. Most of the time, what I would see in the spirit was ministering angels, but there were times that I would sense and see dark spirits. One day, we had received our shipment of go-karts, and we were doing some finishing touches on the guardrail system; two men came into the park. At the time I had no idea who they were or what they were doing there. They just started walking around the park, looking at different things and talking among themselves. When I approached them, they said that they were in the process of breaking ground and building a similar outdoor recreation facility across town. The one man said to me that he was sorry that he was going to put me out of business so quickly, but against this particular franchise that he was building I really didn't have a chance.

Of course deception is going to try to put doubt in my mind as soon as possible, but the thing I knew about the devil was that he will tell you that you cannot have, what God has manifested in our life, and then when he sees that you have it, he'll tell you can't keep it. He will try to get you to question whether or not it was God who gave you the idea or the blessing in the first place. When that man threatened me, he didn't know was that Goliath had taunted the Israelites and told them that he was going to feed their carcasses to the birds of the air. He stood before them and made threats that in the natural were logical, just like this franchise that was going to put this little mom-and-pop establishment out of business. What this man did not understand was that we were not building a financial business; we were being obedient to the most high God, and just like the children of Israel, there were far more with us than there were with him.

That night when I came to the Lord in prayer, he said to me, "Stand fast. There are many battles that you will face, and before you are done, you will slay many giants, you will lay them to rest, and when you are through, there will be little more than a remnant left of their existence."

During the first year of our business, my wife and I learned many things. We found out that being a young married couple with small kids and a business was much harder to maintain then we made it look. There is a saying about ducks on the water, that on top they look very calm and in control, but underneath they're paddling for everything they're worth; that was my wife and me. My wife was doing everything she could to maintain a successful military career and still be a sufficient wife, mother, and Christian business owner. I was doing my best to try to support my wife and her military career and still keep up with being a husband, dad, active member of our church, and business owner. What people on the outside could never understand was the sacrifice that my wife, my kids, and I made on a daily basis so that this new business could continue to run smoothly. My wife and I often struggled to find time for each other, and because of this we often didn't see eye to eye, but what we didn't know was that God was strengthening us to rely more on him and trust him. He was the glue that was going to hold everything together, and without him everything would fall apart. We felt as if we had spiritual battles manifesting around us in a multitude of ways.

Chapter 12: Old Injuries

Years before when I was in the military and had suffered a severe injury to my leg after a car bomb incident, they told me it was possible that I may lose part of my leg below my knee. The doctors had also told me while I was in Germany that due to the metal fragments that went through my lower leg, I would always have problems with blood circulation and possibly blood clots. I had no question that God had healed me and allowed me to keep the limbs that I was born with, but that didn't mean that at some point in time the devil wouldn't come back and test me just to see just where my faith was concerning healings. As it turned out, this was one of those times; maybe it was due to all the long days that I had put in building the go-kart track, or maybe it was just because I was on my feet so much once the track had opened and was actually running. But either way I started having a problem in my lower ankle; a sore had developed, and over time it became a hole in the side of my ankle. Then the hole grew so large that you could place the end of your thumb into the sore so far that you would lose sight of your thumbnail.

Asking for time off when you're the boss in the first year of a new business is almost impossible, but I knew that I couldn't put this off for very long. I went to a doctor on the military base and they proceeded to do the best that they could under the circumstances. They told me that if it didn't start improving, it was possible gangrene may set in. I knew exactly what that meant: amputation. God had healed me one time, and he is the same yesterday, today, and forever. So I knew that if he healed me back when I was in the burn ward in Germany, he could heal me now in New Mexico. The hole in my leg was so painful that in order to wear jeans, I had to roll up that pant leg so that nothing would rub up against it; even the material of my pants caused me a great deal of pain. Some of my staff members thought I was trying to create a new fashion statement by leaving one pant leg rolled up and the other rolled down. On the occasion that a staff member or a customer would see the hole in my leg, they would for some reason ask me the same ridiculous question: Does that hurt? In answer to my prayers, a new physician came to the base that was familiar with my condition. She referred me to a doctor downtown that had a great deal of success in wound care. He told me that most of the time he had seen patients with this type of an injury, it often ended in amputation. But he said, "Before that happens, I will do everything within my power to try to save your lower leg." He proceeded to clean out the injury, which meant removing all of the infected substance; this was not pleasant, but it was necessary. Then he proceeded to pack the injury with a type of antibiotic, filled the hole with gauze, and put my entire lower leg in a soft cast. I worked the go-kart track for many weeks with this soft cast on my lower leg, and within a few months of this process, we started seeing positive results. According to my doctor I was lucky that we got it when we did, because if we had waited longer, his procedure would not have had any effect. According to him, either by incredible timing or the hand of God my lower leg would remain attached and I was again healed by the grace of God.

At our annual men's advance, my role in the event started to become more and more defined as to what the pastors wanted of me. For me it was always easy to tell the pastors all of the wonderful things that I was able to see in the supernatural realm concerning different types of angels and God's blessings being poured out. But what was always hard for me to do was to explain to them how sometimes dark entities would show up and try to sidetrack what it was that God was trying to manifest during their time to speak to the men. My nature is to be an encourager, but I've always struggled when God would ask me to perform some type of spiritual correction. Luckily for me, most of the time, the words the Lord would give me were encouraging and uplifting, but dark entities would show up in all of our lives at one point in time or another. I am simply a commentator on the football field of life; I can only call them as I see them. I have never been good at making things up or faking things. I would rather tell people I have nothing at all or that I'm not seeing anything in the spirit as opposed to making things up on my own. If anything, I struggle at times articulating what it is that I am seeing in the spirit, so I would rather minimize what I see as opposed to stretching the truth. Most of the time when I would go to our men's advances, I would see many of the same things; ceilings and walls in the buildings would simply fade away in the supernatural realm. They would be replaced sometimes with large balconies that would form around the entire seating area, and thousands of angels would look on, talking among themselves and sometimes pointing down, as if to direct the attention of other angels to specific men worshipping during the service.

During some points of the service ministering angels would mingle among the men, sometimes even worshipping God and lifting their hands in the air right next to some of the men. The pastors would often ask me questions about these ministering angels that were among us, because they would take a head count of all the men who were supposed to be there at the men's advance, and without fail the head count of the men who were sitting in the seats was always far more than the people who had bought tickets for the event. As I would look around the sanctuary while the pastors were giving their message, I would see these men sitting among us, and their faces seemed to shine. They would sometimes glance at me as if to acknowledge the fact that they knew I could pick them out; some would even put their index finger in front of their mouth as if to ask me to stay quiet and allow them to sit among the men during the service. Probably 50 percent of what God would allow me to see in the spirit, I would keep to myself; only things that were relevant either to the pastors or men in the congregation would I speak about. It was never my intention to try to entertain anybody as to what I was seeing in the spirit but only to inform them and strengthen their walk with the Lord, or at times to let them know that God was aware of them and that there were ministering angels working in their behalf. I have never been to a men's advance that God didn't move. These events that I'm asked to go to are most often the highlights of my year; I call them "spiritual Super Bowls." When men or women gathered together in Jesus's name and they have an expectancy for God to move in their midst, God will always exceed their expectations and take them to levels they never thought possible.

Phase Two

The first year in our new business went extremely well, and God had put on our hearts that the next thing we were to build that following year was a batting cage. The odd thing for my wife and me was that there was already a batting cage on the south side of town, but it was an older business. The new batting cage systems were automated and worked off computer systems; about all we had to do was watch the people and make sure they had the proper equipment and didn't hurt themselves. My wife and I prayed about this new building project we were to undertake because it was never our intention to compete with any other business. All we knew is that God kept circling back around to this batting cage idea, so that fall after opening the go-kart track as phase one, phase two would be building a batting cage. Once again everyone told us that this was not going to work because there was already an older batting cage business on the south side of town, not to mention a new franchise business that was going to open in the coming spring. So again, my wife and I stepped out of the boat and into faith as we proceeded to secure a new loan to build phase two of our business. I'm not really even sure that our feet had dried from the first time we stepped out of the boat during the building of phase one, but here we were again standing in faith, trusting God.

The process of building the batting cage went incredibly smoothly, and before we knew it, it was up and functioning perfectly. Because it was automated, it was incredibly easy to run, and now we had a small building that was built with the batting cage that turned out to be my family's home away from home for many years. The front half of the building was for business purposes like batting cage bats and helmets as well as a snack bar for customers, but the back room was for family. We had a TV and VCR for the kids as well as an oversize couch and toy boxes to keep my little business partners occupied and happy. My three little sidekicks were extremely good at keeping themselves occupied with their trusty dog and a seven-acre field to play in; there was always something to do. We built a playhouse on the back of one of the billboard signs up by the highway. The billboard sign was still within the fenced in area of the park, so without leaving the grounds, they could go play in their makeshift treehouse. In comparison to how I grew up as a kid, I felt that our three little ones had a pretty incredible life, and even though their mom and dad worked some pretty insane hours, they had no trouble keeping themselves entertained.

As the first season with the batting cage began, a brand-new season of spiritual warfare would begin as well. All my wife and I knew is that

God had put on our hearts to build everything that we had built to this point, and it was very clear to us that not everyone would approve of what we were doing. I was reminded in prayer that not everyone approved of what Noah had been doing, either, and like us many people made fun of him and told him that he was crazy. I knew that there were many things that God had asked people in the Bible to do that seemed crazy at the time, but as God began to unfold the meaning, they weren't crazy at all but fit into his plan for their life. We knew that just because God had called us to walk in faith in our business, there would still be battles to face. In this particular year of business, we were to face one battle and one giant; both were like mountains set before us in our path, but God once again asked us to trust him and walk in faith.

When the franchise business across town opened for business, we were told over and over that it was only a matter of time before we were put out of business; we were only able to build our business in phases, where they were able to build the entire business at one time. People from our church as well as friends and the community told us again and again that it was so unfortunate that we decided to build our business when we did because our timing was so bad. I had faith that God's timing is always perfect, and even though people would always give their opinion, we were to love those same people and trust the Lord. Financially, that year turned out not to be very good for us. My wife and I felt we had done everything that we were supposed to do, but because we lived in a small town and there were now three facilities that people had to choose from, there was only so much money to be made.

Our church had been in a building project for some time, and we were in the process of moving to the new location as well as a much larger building and sanctuary. In the body of Christ, if things are strong and healthy, they grow, and our church was no exception. Not only did the church flourish, but they were able to hire more pastors and staff members. Our new associate pastor and I were asked at times to go out to members of the church who were struggling with different types of dark entities. At one such meeting, we were asked to go to a couple's house. The husband didn't really attend the church, but the wife was an active member. She had been having trouble for quite some time, and things at home were just getting worse. She asked if the associate pastor and I could come visit her husband and see if we could determine anything going on with him spiritually speaking. My wife was friends with the woman and asked if she could come along with us so that the woman from our church wouldn't be the only female in the room. When the associate pastor, my wife, and I arrived, we sat down in the living room with the husband and wife. The conversation started out fairly normally, and in the spirit, I did not see anything unusual, but I did sense things moving around in the room.

After about twenty minutes or so, the associate pastor looked at me and said, "Are you sensing anything in the room that we need to know about?"

I didn't reply to his question immediately. I turned to look at the husband, and I noticed the silhouette of a head peering out from behind his head. Still not saying anything, the husband started to grin at me in a very uneasy way. As I was seeing this manifesting with him, my curiosity grew.

Still looking at the husband, I said, "So just how many demonic entities are with you?"

Opening his mouth as wide as he could but still smiling, he said, "Why don't you tell me, seer?"

At that point God allowed me to see things much clearer, and I saw three dark entities with him, but only one was attached. Seeing demonic entities was something I was used to, and for the most part, I could even identify the demonic entities that I was dealing with. The dominant entity began to address me in a deep and sinister manufactured voice, no doubt trying to create fear in the associate pastor, my wife, and me. I can't speak for the other people in the room, but I was not entertained. The first words out of my mouth were to direct the demonic entity who was addressing me speak to in normal tones, in Jesus's name. At that point, the voice became much quieter, just above the sound of a whisper.

I looked at the associate pastor, who had a smile on his face and said, "You're doing great; just keep going."

I looked back at the husband, and I said, "In Jesus's name I cast you out; you have no place here."

The two minor demonic entities left immediately, and the one who had spoken to me from behind the husband's head came out of the man and manifested almost like a boa constrictor that had coiled itself around this man's torso. The man's wife, who had been crying, left the room and my wife accompanied her out. The associate pastor and I were left with this man and his demonic entity, and he for some reason decided to start confessing everything he had ever done against anybody, including his wife. The more he talked, the more the grip that the demonic entity had on this husband began to loosen. Soon the entity returned back to its actual size and shape and just sat on the floor next to the husband. The man began to break and cry. He said that he was so sorry for all the things he had done to deceive everyone but most of all his wife. His wife had heard everything from the next room and was mortified as to all of the activities that her husband had been taking part in. My wife was doing her best to calm her down and remind her that her husband was trying to confess his sins so that God may forgive him.

Quietly under my breath, I looked at the little demonic entity sitting on the floor next to him and said once again, "In Jesus's name, I cast you out. You have no place here; you must leave."

With that he exited the room. Where he went, I have no idea, but the man who was left sitting in the chair was physically and mentally broken. The pastor and I went over to him and began to pray with him. He had so many questions that needed to be answered, and the pastor assured him that if he was sincere, God would cast his sins into the sea of forgetfulness. But the man's wife in the other room said that she didn't think there was any way she could ever forgive him of all the deception, all of the adultery. For many weeks afterward, we followed up with the husband and wife, and he started a slow journey coming back to the presence of God. There were many times that we had to cast the demons out because they kept coming back to him in later days, but he learned that he had authority himself and could overcome them with the help of the Lord Jesus and was eventually set free. His wife, on the other hand, struggled with forgiveness and felt that she could never trust him again. Even though they are not together, they have both found grace and forgiveness and still serve God to this day.

Hailstones from Heaven

Once again in the spring, our churches men's advance was upon us. I am sure I could tell story after story about these men's meetings, but one particular story still stands out in my mind. It was on a Friday night, and the presence of God was very strong in this service. When you get hundreds of men together and they are all worshipping God of one accord, in those times God moves! We were singing a praise and worship song, and one of the best things about the men's event was nobody really cared how good or bad you could sing; we were just singing to the Lord. In the spirit I could see large, heavy chains draped over many of the men. The chains were heavy and weighed them down, and as they sang to the Lord in the spirit, I could see the chains starting to melt and run down the frames of their bodies until they reached the floor. The chains didn't just pile up on the floor; slowly they started to melt into the floor.

As I was watching this happen, an angel of the Lord appeared in front of me and held out his hand. He said, "Come with me and see."

I put my hand in his hand, and when I did, I was no longer standing in the sanctuary with hundreds of men; I had been given a vision of a compartment in hell. The angel that had stood before me in the sanctuary was still standing in front of me, but his wings had become transparent so that I was able to see straight through them like glass. As I peered through his wing, I could feel heat, like when you stand too close to a large bonfire, and to be safe you feel like you have to take a few steps back so that you won't get singed by the heat. I could smell something like burnt hair and sulfur, and when I looked up, I could see these chains that had been wrapped around the men in the sanctuary draping down from somewhere up above like stalactites. I could still hear the men in the sanctuary faintly singing, and as they did, there were large white hailstones about the size of bowling balls barreling down into this compartment of hell. On the ground all around the area that I could see were these demonic entities doing their best to cover their heads from the impacts of these bowling-ball-size hailstones. They were screaming and crying out and scurrying about as best they could to get out of the way, and still faintly, I could hear the men's voices singing. The words that they sang were so powerful, and with their words, they were able to break free from the bondage that had been heaped upon them by way of the dark spirits and their master. Still looking through the angel's wing that was in front of me, I was able to look even further into a compartment of hell, as if there were binoculars to increase my ability to see further. There was one particular compartment that held what I thought was a small demonic entity; in fact, the prince of lies himself was crumpled up like a ball sitting on the ground with one eye peering out, watching the barrage of hailstones.

Just then the angel that was standing before me said, "It's time for us to go back."

In the blink of an eye, I was standing back in the sanctuary with the men as they were singing praises to the Lord, and as I looked around, I could see the balconies of angels and the ministering spirits moving among the men. There was a cloud up where the ceiling in the sanctuary should have been, and I could see the cloud still rotating slowly like the eye of the storm.

I asked myself, "How do I explain to these men of God where I was taken and what I have seen?"

I could still feel the heat on my skin and smell the smells that were all around me while I was in the bowels of the earth. Later I talked to my pastor about what I had seen and where I had been taken. At this point in my walk with the Lord, I was much more comfortable telling my pastor about the things that I had seen and allowing him to tell my stories because he was far better at conveying what it was I was seeing to the men.

By now God had opened my eyes many times and showed me so many things that I couldn't possibly remember them all, but my vision at the men's advance was the first time that I believe I was shown things in the spirit and felt like I was actually there.

Vision of Heaven

On returning from the mountain, I would move back into my normal routine. I had been praying with our pastor on Wednesdays, Thursdays, and Fridays for quite some time. My pastor and I had prayed over the years, sometimes for as much as two or three hours consecutively. God had sent to me a ministering spirit to confirm that this was part of the reason that my wife and I were brought here in the middle of the desert. I also felt that my pastor was put into my life to be a spiritual mentor, strengthening me in places that I was deficient before. He enjoyed allowing different men from the church to come in and pray with us, and for the most part, that was generally a good thing, but every now and then, men would come in to our prayer settings and just wanted to have general conversations. It was sometimes so distracting that I would stop praying with the pastors because at times I felt I was more effective praying for them on my own at home. It usually wasn't long before my pastor would find me and asked me why I stopped coming to prayer. I never wanted to point out any person, but my pastor was a wise man and generally knew my answer before I said it; often, he had sensed the same thing as well. I was still quiet about most things, but my pastor knew me well enough to know when spiritual things were affecting our prayer time. Most of the time, the people who just wanted to have everyday conversations would get tired of coming to prayer when they finally realized that the rest of us were not there to socialize. It took time to gather the prayer warriors and gently weed out the visitors. Once it was understood that we were in this place to seek God's word and his presence, God began to do incredible things through our pastor's prayer group.

My day was always full, but making time for prayer time was a vital part of my week. Only after my prayer time was completed and I had finished my daily workout would I go to work at our business. On average, I worked ten hours a day, seven days a week, as well as getting the kids back and forth from school and after-school events. God had often used the quietest part of my day, which was weight training in my home, to speak to me. Yes, he would speak to me in my prayer time as well, but for some reason when I was lifting weights, my mind was often very quiet. One morning when I was beginning a chest-and-triceps routine, an angel appeared in the room. This had happened to me before, but as a general rule, the angel wouldn't really talk to me much.

But on this particular morning, the angel once again said to me, "Take my hand." And he held out his hand.

I was sitting on the edge of my bench in the weight room and being compliant. I held out my hand and took hold of the outstretched hand in front of me. As soon as I did, I was taken to a place that to me smelled like orange blossoms and honeysuckle, just like my home where I grew up as a kid in Southern California. The angel and I were standing in a field next to a stream, and as we walked in this field, the blades of grass looked like they were standing up under our weight, not leaving any footprints behind us.

I looked at the stream next to us, and the angel asked, "Would you like to put your hand in?"

I didn't answer, but I knelt down on one knee and put my hand into what I thought was water. When I scooped my hand out, it was more like tiny little diamond chips rolling along this stream, and when I poured it back in, my hand was not wet at all. I looked back to the angel that was walking with me, and he just smiled. On the other side of the river, there was a large mountain, and it had snow on it that came all the way down to the other side of the stream.

I looked back to the angel, and he said to me, “You can walk to the foot of the mountain if you want to touch the snow.”

I said to the angel, “But there is no bridge to cross over the stream.”

He smiled a wide smile and said, “Go ahead; you can walk across it.”

I took a step onto the stream, and as the angel had said, it supported my weight. I walked to the foot of the mountain that had snow on it, and when I dipped my hand into the snow, it wasn’t cold at all. It compacted like snow, and when I made a snowball and threw it at the mountain, it acted like snow. The angel, still with a grin on his face, just looked at me as if I were a child doing something that amused him. I walked back across the stream to the field on the other side. As I was looking around, there were animals there, and about ten feet behind me were some of my household pets that I had grown up with, as well as one that had just passed away a year before.

The angel said to me, “Do you recognize them?”

I said, “Absolutely!”

There were extremely large trees, and the odd thing was that there was no shade under the tree. As we passed under the tree, the leaves had no shade on the bottoms.

The angel, as if knowing what I was thinking at the time, said, "God's light is everywhere in this place, and there are no shadows."

As we kept walking, I began to see people gathered in groups, some by the stream and others under the large trees. As we began to get closer to them, the person who was leading the group would call out my name as if he knew me. For some reason, at that moment, I knew the person's name who had called out to me, and the group would smile and wave. Many of the people in the group were wearing a type of gown, and the person who appeared to be leading the group was wearing what I would call a robe.

I asked the angel who was guiding me, "Why are they dressed differently?"

He said, "The ones that are dressed in gowns are being taught the word of God. They had been born again into the body of Christ but had not been taught the word of God, and in some cases, they had died in their earthly bodies prematurely and were being raised by angelic beings and the saints. The robes that you see are the robes of righteousness. They are the teachers of God's word. Some of them are the saints of old, and others are the New Testament saints."

I looked farther into the distance. I could see a great ocean, and the stream that we had been walking next to ran into it. There were large houses and streets that shone in the light.

The angel said to me, "Would you like to see the house that has been prepared for you?"

I replied to him, "I don't think I am ready for that, but thank you for the offer."

He smiled at me again and said, "Come with me; there is someone that wants to have a word with you."

I followed him back into a grassy area with flowers as far as the eyes could see, and off in the distance, I could see a group of what looked like people walking. The angel that was with was very excited about where we were going, and the group that was off in the distance was walking straight to us. The closer the group in the distance came, the more I felt like there was a weight on me, like gravity was somehow failing me and I was being pulled to the ground.

I asked the angel that was with me, "Why do I feel like I'm having trouble walking the closer this group comes to us?" Looking up, I still couldn't make out who was in the group.

The angel said, "Sometimes when people are brought before the Lord for the first time, this is common."

Feeling like my head was very heavy, I looked up once again, and what I thought was a group of people was actually a host of angels, some walking and some hovering above the ground. I couldn't really see the face of the man who was walking in the middle, and the closer the group came, I felt like gravity was forcing me to my knees.

The angel put his hand on my left shoulder and asked, "Are you OK?"

I said, "I don't know what's wrong, but I know I can't get up from here."

He said, "Don't fight it. Just do what you can."

As the group drew even closer, I lay down on my stomach flat on the ground with my head to one side.

All I could see were some feet and sandals with robes covering most of their feet. One of them came down on one knee and touched my right shoulder and said, "In time you will be able to stand in my presence, but for now, I just want you to listen."

He said to me, "Give my people one message: tell them that I am proud of what they are doing in the Father's name. Tell them that if I was to hang on the cross for just one of them, that they would have been worth it, just you, just one of them would have been worth the price that I had to pay.

Go and tell them that there is a place here for them, each and every one of them that chooses to believe."

The one who was knelt down next to me speaking stood up, and the group went on past. After a few minutes had passed, I was able to stand up, but my physical body felt exhausted. The angel led me back to what looked like a park, and I sat down on a bench with the angel still standing in front of me.

In what felt like the blink of an eye, I was sitting on my weight bench preparing to start my chest-and-triceps workout. I looked at the clock on the wall, and only a couple of minutes had passed. I was still on schedule to finish my lift and get to the church on time for the pastor's prayer before going to work. Before I had the vision when I was at the men's advance on the mountain and now having a vision in my weight room before I trained, these were things that were not common to me. I had been seeing in the spirit since I was a child, and I wasn't one to even remember my dreams, but the visions that God had shown me over the past few months were so real to me. There were things in my visions that I could touch and smell, and they were incredibly tangible. The sounds of voices and gentle breezes were also existent and were things I had never experienced before in my walk with the Lord, but these events were true and as real as my day-to-day life.

Chapter 13: A New Assignment

In the fall after we had built the batting cage, my wife and I decided that we would leave the military base-housing unit and buy a travel trailer to live in at the park. We were able to purchase a large trailer so that each one of our three kids had their own bed as well as a master bedroom for my wife and me. We had moved our washer and dryer into the ticket booth for the go-kart track at the park so that we would have a place on site that we could do laundry; since the kids were still small, it actually worked out very well. I was able to get a lot of work done at the park, and because my wife was still in the military, I was able to use the base fitness center to work out in the mornings.

Coexisting with the new outdoor recreation facility across town was difficult, and one morning after coming home from the gym on base, I decided to walk around in the field to the north of our travel trailer, just walking and praying and seeking God's wisdom on how we were to face the newest mountain that was before us. As I was walking, I looked down and saw an old golf putter lying on the ground. It was almost dead center in the middle of the park; it would have been impossible for somebody to stand outside the fence and throw it that far, or it would have damaged the antique putter. I stood in front of it facing north and bent over to pick it up as I stood up, and angel stood before me.

The angel reminded me that when he had come to me before, I looked like Noah had looked when he was building the ark. Then the angel said, "But now the Lord says that you will be my David. An enemy of the Lord has come against you, just as the Philistines stood against David and his people. The putter that you hold in your hand is your sling, and with it you will defeat your Goliath."

Holding the putter in my hand, I said to the angel, "I'm supposed to build a miniature golf course?"

My wife and I had been given a loan for the original go-kart track, and then we had gone back to the bank to get more money for the batting cage. My question wasn't whether or not we should build a miniature golf course, because that made sense; what I wasn't sure about was where we would get the money to build it.

The angel, knowing what I was thinking, said, "Trust in the Lord your God."

I understood the orders that I was given, but I didn't know how I was going to convey these orders to my wife, who was extremely good with finances. So that morning I walked around the field with an old putter in my hand, praying for favor with the bank and with my wife as well because explaining this to both of them and getting approved may have been a miracle in itself. I proceeded to talk to my wife, who agreed with me that this would be a logical next step and said when God manifests the money, then we would begin to build phase three of our business. We went to the bank that had given us the loans for the go-kart track and the batting cage, and they were unwilling to extend us anymore credit due to the year we had after building the batting cage. I believe they felt with this new franchise in town, it was only a matter of time before we defaulted on our loan. They said that if we were to build the miniature golf course, we would have to find another way to produce the finances.

My wife is a type of person who, if she is sure that God is moving things, is going to find a way to make things happen. She is an incredible woman of faith. Her solution to our problem was way outside the box as far as conventional business funding. What my wife decided was that we could use our credit cards that gave us checks to fund the building of the miniature golf course. Using sixteen different credit cards that totaled up to $200,000, we proceeded to build our miniature golf course during the fall and through the winter. We had placed hole one in the exact spot that I had found the old antique putter, and even when the construction process was going on, there were always ministering angels walking around the golf course.

At first, I felt like they were there to reassure my wife and me that we were walking in faith as to what God had placed on our hearts and almost every day. I would go out on the golf course to see if the angels would speak to me. They were generally talking among themselves, and for the most part, they would just smile at me and go about their business. At times there was as many as one hundred or so out there strolling around the grounds. I would even look out the window of our trailer at night and see them shining in the darkness.

Oddly enough, I had never really seen very many angels at the go-kart track or the batting cage, but on the golf course, it was a whole different thing. Maybe it was because we had extended ourselves so far in trusting God. For the golf course, we didn't just step out of the boat; we lost sight of the boat, and the shore was nowhere to be seen. Obviously, my wife and I had very good credit, and why we had so many credit cards between us, I still have no idea. But now we were going to have to make our business loan payment as well as sixteen credit card payments. So we went into our third year of business and had completed phase three of the building process. Each and every day that we opened our gates, we trusted that God was going to bring us a miracle and allow us to overcome the giants as well as the mountains that had been placed before us. The angel had told me that I was no longer going to resemble Noah, but I was going to be like David, a slayer of giants.

In the year to come, the franchise that the bank, the people in my church, and my friends had told me was going to put my wife and me out of business—the one that everyone told us we couldn't survive against—went out of business. The truth is, I knew what God had placed on my heart, to slay Goliath, but on the other side of this battlefield, there were real people. God had also put it on my heart to pray for them every single day when I drove past their business, and as hard as it was to do that, I can truthfully say that I did. I didn't know them, and I didn't know their families; I only slightly knew what they looked like, but God knew their hearts inside and out. He knew every hair on their heads. I would lift them up by name and pray that God would touch their hearts, and I believe, without any question, that he did. I knew that someday soon, these people whom God had placed on my heart would come to be my brother and sister in Christ. I can now say that God manifested the prayers that he had placed in me, and to this day these people are in truth my brother and sister in Christ.

Before long we were the only go-kart, batting cage, and miniature golf offering within one hundred miles of our business. At some point the batting cage on the south end of town had gone out of business as well, and for a season we prospered and were able to pay off some of the sixteen credit cards and consolidate all existing debt into one payment. God is good on so many levels, and his timing is perfect. There was always a sense of peace and tranquility in that area of the park. It was always my special place to go and pray and be among these ministering angels—not really to talk to them but just to glorify God with them, praising him for the things he had done in my life and for my family.

Divine Appointment

It goes without saying that in order to win the battle, you have to admit that you are in a war. Before we could even celebrate the victory that we had just witnessed, a new battle showed up on my horizon. It was familiar to me, and I had faced this same enemy several times before. Any time that I would suffer an injury to my lower leg, there was always the possibility that if it wasn't taken care of quickly, it would get out of control. And like before, a hole had opened up on my ankle, but this time it was the size of a silver dollar, and the doctor who had been able to repair and reverse the damage was not having the same results using the same procedures. My doctor was basically waiting for a time to amputate. Since the pain had gotten so bad, I could no longer walk on my leg, and my wife and I went to buy a set of crutches at the local medical supply store. Little did we know it was a divine appointment.

The lady running the store asked when we were going to go see a wound specialist and said that she knew of a really good one in Texas. We told her that we had never heard of such a doctor and that we would definitely take his name and make an appointment straightaway. The facility we contacted ended up being a Christian-run clinic, and God had just sent us the advice and help we needed.

When my wife and I arrived at the appointment, they had already received the scans as well as the reports on my ankle, so they had a good idea what it was they were looking at. When they removed the soft cast, I thought to myself that this was the worst I had seen my ankle look since the original injury. When my local doctor sent down my files, he also sent a series of pictures as to the progression and regression of my injury to my ankle. They decided to go ahead and inject me with dye and perform scans on my veins. When they took me into the room where I was to get my scan, I sat on the table and quietly began to pray. I had been healed several times before, and in my mind, I wasn't ready to lose my leg. I sat there for a few minutes just praying and thanking God for another victory of healing in my leg.

When the nurse walked into the room, she said to me, “Are you believing for a miracle?”

I answered, “Yes, I am believing for a miracle.”

She said, “Then I will pray and believe with you.” And she did.

The tech that was to perform the procedure and one of the doctors stood at the door waiting for us to finish praying. When the nurse and I both looked up, they entered the room and completed the scan.

The nurse came back to me later and said, “We’re going to take you back to the room while the doctors look at the results to see how they’re going to proceed.”

I looked at her. I said, “In Jesus’s name, I am not losing my leg.” The nurse and my wife agreed.

My wife held my hand while we were waiting for the doctors to come back into the room. We didn’t say much; we just prayed under our breath quietly. I just thanked God for the miracle that I knew he was about to perform. When the doctors came into the room, they carried with them the scan from the week earlier as well as the one that they had just taken an hour before, and they placed them on a viewing area that was on the wall. Truthfully, I didn’t really know what they were looking at, but obviously it was extremely significant to them.

They said, "This is the picture that was taken a week ago, where you can see that many of the veins had either shut down or had collapsed. Now this is the scan we took today, and what it looks like is that your leg has redirected the blood flow, and it appears that you have sufficient blood flow back to your ankle and foot area. So for right now, due to the fact that your blood flow has increased, we feel that the area that has opened up on your leg should heal just fine."

I would love to say that my wife and I were overjoyed about the news but in my heart, I knew that they were going to come back with a good report. I know how powerful our words are, and in Jesus's name, I knew I had the victory, and I had to do a better job of taking care of my leg.

Praying was something that most Christians are familiar with, but most view it as a last resort when things are falling apart in their life. For some people it just comes naturally in their day-to-day lives, and for others it can be difficult. For me praying was always one of the more natural aspects of serving God. No one really needed to tell me that I need to pray; I have just always enjoyed that part of being a Christian. I always felt that giving up my own personal time to pray with my pastor was like sowing seed into incredibly good soil. Most of the people I prayed with were pastors who were on staff, and it was a part of their day. God would speak to them and give the revelation as to how they were to move forward and prosper in ministries that they were to oversee at the church. Many of the days that I would go to pray, I was paying an employee to cover my shift so that I would not miss this important part of my day. One of the things a ministering angel told me was that I was put in this position to allow this particular pastor to mentor me. I was also given an assignment to pray with him, and the Lord would use me and my gift to assist him in his ministry.

My pastor has always made it known to me that he enjoys praying with a seer. In one of the prayer meetings, two other pastors from our church were present, and a specific angel appeared in the room. It was, of course, common for me to see ministering angels during our prayer sessions, but this particular angel asked me a question. The reason why this was relevant is because I would frequently see ministering angels, but it wasn't often that they spoke to me.

This angel said to me, "Seer, what is it specifically that you and your brothers in Christ seek?"

I answered the angel and asked, "Can you be more specific as to what you mean?"

The angel replied, "What are the desires of your heart?"

I relayed this information to the other three pastors in the room, that one by one, quietly to themselves; they were to speak out the desires of their heart. The first pastor began to quietly, under his breath, ask God for the manifestations of things that he and his wife desired. As soon as he was done, the second pastor, also quietly under his breath, spoke out what it was that he and his family desired. Then my pastor, with a much longer list than the other two, spoke out things that he and his family as well as the church was believing for. As each one of the pastors was speaking, there were ministering angels coming and going. I believe that by the pastors' words, they were putting the ministering angels on assignment.

Then the angel turned to me and said, "Seer, what is it that you desire?"

And just like the pastors, quietly under my breath, I spoke the words that I believed would manifest in Jesus's name.

When we were all finished, the angel looked at me and said, "You and the pastors ask for so little."

When I shared this with the other men in the room, they all laughed and said, "We thought we were asking way beyond anything we could ever imagine."

We tend to look at things through a small keyhole and say to ourselves, "These are the blessings we are believing for," but God not only opens the door to what we are believing, but he also removes the wall and asks, "Just how much can you trust me to manifest in your lives by faith?"

Sometimes the pastors asked me to sit in on meetings with church members basically so that I could give them a play-by-play as to what is manifesting in the spirit. On one occasion I was with one of the pastors, and they had a meeting scheduled with a single mom and one of her children. The child, who was hiding under the furniture during the entire meeting, would not speak to either the pastor or me.

The only thing the child would say was, "When can we get out of here?"

The mother, who was clearly at the end of her rope because of events that had happened at the church and at school, was unclear on which way to turn. For the most part, I sat quietly listening to one of the staff pastors do their best to try to help the mother. The pastor and I were able to give the mother several scriptures to stand on as well as pray with her. We made sure that she knew that she had dominion over any of these dark spirits that were causing turmoil in her home. We also informed her that whenever possible, she should pray over her child as often as she felt necessary, that she could take authority over anything that was causing the child to act in a way that was disrespectful to her and the faculty at school. There was also an entity of deception that was putting thoughts in her mind, thoughts of things that on her own, she didn't agree with, but because she believed that these things were coming to her were her own thoughts, she received them. The truth was this dark spirit was being allowed to take her down a path that she really didn't want to go.

When the staff pastor and I finished the meeting and the mother and the child had left, the pastor said to me, "There were certain things that you didn't address that I really thought you would."

I said, "Are you referring to the demonic entity that was causing the child to act up during the meeting?"

The staff pastor answered and said, "So there was a demon with them."

I said, "Of course there was, but what the ministering angel spoke to me was if the mother heard this, it would've pushed her over the edge, because she was contemplating suicide by way of this dark entity of deception. What I was told in the spirit was that if this had been revealed, the parent may have gone home, injured the child, and then taken her own life. That is why I continued to emphasize that she had authority over all dark spirits and, if need be, multiple times a day, to bind them and cast them out in Jesus's name. Also, the fact that the thoughts that were in her mind were not her ideas but they were lies placed there by an evil spirit."

The staff pastor said, "For some reason I knew there was a lot more to the story that you were not saying, but I understand now why you handled it the way you did."

Business, Family, Rentals, and another TDY

By this time, my wife and I had acquired several rental properties and also continued to maintain our outdoor recreation business, and my wife's military career was going well. Our daughters were both in school, and my son was still following me around doing his best to help his dad maintain everything. Things were running smoothly when a new set of orders came down for my wife informing her that she would be going overseas for a one-year remote assignment that was to be unaccompanied by her family. All I knew was that for the next year, I was going to be a single parent to my three kids as well as having to keep up with the rental properties and run the family business. The good thing was that by this time, my marriage was stronger than ever, and my walk with God was strong as well. I knew that not only was God going to get me through this next year, but he was going to be with my wife, strengthening her as well. Sometimes God puts us in situations that we don't always understand, but in the overall picture they are necessary.

A year earlier a good friend of mine was going through a tough time in his life, and my wife and I had invited him to stay with us at our house. From the outside looking in, it looked as if we were being a blessing to this friend of ours from church, but in many ways when my wife left on her one-year assignment overseas, our houseguest became someone whom I would learn to lean on. My kids would even refer to him as their uncle, and at a time in my life that I really did need a brother, he became just that: a brother. He was someone whom I could depend on and trust with my kids, and he even helped me with many of the chores around the house. He was a lousy cook, but he was great at bringing home takeout food. We had actually become friends playing softball for the church, and our friendship was strengthened when we became workout partners in the gym.

He would say, "Iron sharpens iron."

My wife and I talked nearly every single day that she was gone. Whether by phone or computer, we stayed in contact and never truly left each other's side. I believe in this time that we were apart; we grew so much stronger as a couple and realized that we actually did need each other more than we knew. While my wife was overseas, a property became available on the foreclosed market, and as if I didn't have enough on my plate, we ended up buying the property, which had two rental properties that went along with it. This was perfect for my friend from church who had been living with us because it would enable him to have his own house and privacy. While my wife was still overseas, we packed up all of our household goods and moved to another location on the north end of town.

In the second rental house on the property, we were able to bring in a young man from the church that was in need of a rental house. He was the son of the usher whom God had instructed me to talk to when my wife and I first started attending our church many years ago. I knew that God had put this young man in our family's life for many reasons, and just like our friend who had lived with us for so many years, this young man became like a son to my wife and me as well as a big brother to my kids. He had been a good friend of our family for years, and he and his sister were also the first employees I hired in our business several years before. He, too, like his father, was a man of God, and from the first day that he began to work for me, I knew that he was very special in so many ways. He and his sister were not only my best employees, but they were so loyal to my wife and I that they were like our own children.

For quite some time now, my dad had been having trouble with an old car that he had been driving. In the past he had a pickup truck that he put thousands of miles on until it finally gave out on him. Now he and my stepmother were down to one vehicle that was well past its prime. My wife and I decided that we would do our best to honor my dad and stepmom by purchasing them a car. My dad and I had talked back and forth quite a bit, and I was sure I knew what he was looking for, so after shopping around for a few months, my wife and I came across a car that we thought was perfect for them. It was a newer Cadillac that didn't have a lot of miles on it. So we purchased the car and planned a trip to the Midwest, to where my dad and stepmom lived.

My wife and kids piled into our truck, and I drove the Cadillac on the twelve-hour trip. My dad knew that we had been shopping for a car, but he had no idea we were actually driving one back to him. When we showed up at their house, he wasn't really paying attention to what was sitting in his driveway. My wife and the three little ones and I went into the house and immediately went downstairs where my dad was, and as usual my stepmother stayed upstairs doing her best to avoid us. But during the initial conversation, I thought it would be a good idea if my stepmom came downstairs so that we could give them both the news. There was always a sense of tension in my dad and stepmother's house, like a steel trap with a hair trigger that could go off at any moment. For some reason I thought this gesture of goodwill would have a positive effect on a bad relationship between my stepmother and me that had existed since I was a child.

With my three kids ready to burst at the seams wanting to tell their grandpa that we had brought them a car, we handed my dad the keys and informed him that we had brought them something. Demonic entities were very common in this household, and my wife and I were praying quietly under our breath and hoping for the best. My dad was so happy that he couldn't contain himself until he looked at my stepmother, who looked like she had just been blindsided with terrible news. I could see the dark entities starting to move, and I suggested that we go outside and look at the car. We all went out to the driveway, and once again my dad was beside himself with joy.

He asked my stepmom if she wanted to come out and sit on the passenger side to see what she thought, but she replied, "No, this is close enough for me."

At this point my wife and I weren't sure if we had opened a new can of worms to cause increased tension within this already stressful situation, and the smile on my dad's face went from excitement to what looked like concern within minutes. We had told them that we could only stay for a couple of days and then we would have to head back to New Mexico, and the longer we stayed, the more the tension in the house began to escalate. I was pretty sure that if anyone in the family or even a complete stranger gave them a car, they would both be jumping for joy, but because it was my wife and I who tried to bless them with a vehicle, I felt as if it was all my stepmother could do not to scream. I believe for her, just the thought of a car in the driveway that was a gift from me was more than she could bear. After all, she had done everything she could possibly do to destroy my relationship with my dad.

But what she didn't understand was that God's grace and forgiveness were so much bigger than her hatred for me and my family that I was not about to let these dark entities completely ruin the relationship I had with my dad. Looking back, just as God had forgiven me time and time again, I was going to do everything within my power to not only forgive but also be a blessing. Within a few days, my wife and I felt as if we had worn out our welcome once again, and as was with the custom with visiting my dad and stepmom, my dad would apologize for her, and we would be on our way. It was as if the dark entities that she allowed in her life would not only torment her each and every day, but they were also determined that she would have very little joy in her life at all. I had always felt since I was a child that the only reason my stepmother truly hated me so much was because I reminded her of the previous relationship that my dad had with my mother, and she would do anything to remove that memory and me.

Within weeks of returning back home, I received a phone call from my dad telling my wife and me that they were going to have to somehow send the car back to us in New Mexico because my stepmother couldn't tolerate seeing it in the driveway knowing that my wife and I had purchased it. In the two weeks that it was at his house, she had never even sat in it. I felt like somebody had punched me in the stomach, and my wife and I weren't sure how we were going to get the car back to New Mexico because we were not able to take the time off to go back on a second trip. As God would have it, my wife's family would come to the rescue. It was my wife's mother and father who went to my dad's and stepmom's house to pick up the Cadillac. They brought the car back to their house, and it stayed there until two of her sisters had an opportunity to drive it down to New Mexico for us. For me it was extremely embarrassing as to why this even happened, but my wife's parents had always been incredibly kind to me. In some ways, I think they understood the situation with my dad and stepmom.

Back at the church, I was kept busy assisting some of the pastors with meetings that they thought I could help in with people in the congregation, once again leaning on the fact that God often opened my eyes to see in the spirit and would allow me to minister to them on a little bit different level. At one particular meeting that I was asked to sit in on, a woman sat down with me and one of the pastors in the church. The pastors were always careful not to give me any information on the people whom I was to meet with because if God was going to show me things or allow me to see things in the spirit, they didn't want me to have any prior information to dilute what God wanted to do. The woman sat down across from me, and the pastor, who was seated at his desk, told me the woman's name and asked if God had given me anything for her or shown me anything in the spirit. I told the woman that I had sensed that she and her family had gone through an extreme amount of pain over the last year. I also told her that her kids, who had themselves suffered a great loss, were going to find peace and the ability to overcome what had been taken from them. I continued by saying that through God's love and support of her family and church, God was going to restore them and make them whole again.

As she wiped the tears from her eyes and asked me how I knew these things, I told her that all I was doing was repeating what the ministering angel had said and that none of the words were really mine. She said that her husband had suffered a heart attack and the paramedics weren't able to revive him. He wasn't very old, so it was unexpected to her and the rest of the family. In her own words, she alluded to the truth that she had, to some extent, expected something like this to happen. I felt like this was not a good time to tell her that often, God shows us things not to prepare us for bad things to happen, but to pray over them and bind them in Jesus's name so that we can protect ourselves and our family, friends, and loved ones from situations that God wants to protect us from. Many unfortunate things that we experience in our life were never meant to happen, and often by way of our own words, we allow them to manifest. But I do believe that by standing in faith and praying over things, we can deflect many of the fiery arrows of the devil from reaching us or our loved ones.

In another meeting with one of the staff pastors, I was once again asked to sit in to see if God would show me things in the spirit. You have to understand that only when God allows me to see things or know things is it possible for me to have any input, but on many occasions, he does open my eyes in the spirit and allows me to see things that otherwise I would have no way of knowing. As I was sitting in the pastor's office with a young lady, God began to show me a great deal of pain and tragedy that had taken place in this young lady's life. Then I could see in the spirit a dark entity that was trying to silence this young woman from speaking by strangling her; it was as if he was trying to steal her voice. This demonic entity didn't want her to speak the truth; it wanted her silenced. It even went as far as to try to remove her from existence. Silencing her wasn't enough; this entity wanted her dead and was willing to go to great lengths to achieve it. But God had a plan for this young woman's life, a plan that would allow her to survive such a vicious attack from the enemy. God was going to restore her voice and allow her to be a blessing and a witness to many other women. At first the young woman stared at me as if she didn't understand what I was saying, and for a moment I thought that the words that had been given to me were not even close to hitting the mark. Glancing over at the staff pastor who was in the room with me, she began to cry, and for the next few minutes she was unable to speak any words.

When she regained her composure, she looked back at me and said, "Do you know me somehow?"

I said, "I'm sorry; I don't. But God knows you, so if what I have spoken is true, then God is going to use you to speak to many people with an incredible testimony."

She said, "The truth is that several months ago I was attacked by a man, assaulted, strangled, and left for dead. The doctors weren't even sure that I would survive the attack, more or less ever speak again due to the damage that I endured."

She had survived the attack and had been standing in faith, believing for a healing from God, and she had prayed for quite some time that he would restore her voice. Only days before this meeting, her voice supernaturally returned to her. The doctors said it was a miracle that she even lived through the ordeal, let alone returned back to a normal life and the ability to speak. I told her that God had heard her prayers and that by way of her faith, she was completely healed. She still had the scars of this unimaginable experience but possessed an incredible testimony as to God's ability to heal and survive, as well as to encourage many people that have survived similar experiences.

Chapter 14: Dealing with Family

My pastor thought that the experience I had earlier concerning heaven and hell needed to be heard by other people, so he decided to have us sit down and document the entire experience on a DVD. My ability to see into the spirit wasn't a topic of conversation with my wife and me at home and was talked about even less with my three kids. They all understood that I had been given this gift, but to them I was just Dad. I was extremely close to my kids and had played a major part in all of their lives as far as school events and sports activities; most of the time, I was part of their coaching staff. When my oldest daughter started dating, like most fathers, I found this was all new to me. It wasn't like there was any instruction book as to how you were to go about allowing boys to date your daughter. When she was a few years into her teens, she started to hang out more and more with friends, and that included boys as well. She became particularly interested in one boy who attended a very small church in a neighboring town. This particular church operated differently than the church we had attended for many years, the one my daughter was used to. But when you have a fascination for someone, you sometimes let down your spiritual guard and become blind to different things, thinking that it's OK because they still read out of the Bible and that they just interpret it completely differently. In the spirit on occasion, I would see different things with this young man, and I just thought, *He's young, and we all deal with dark entities trying to put thoughts into our minds*. On the occasion that I was around them together and I would see things in the spirit, I would just cast it out in Jesus's name and dismiss it. They dated for quite some time, and my wife and I noticed that more and more often, she started attending the young man's church that in truth we knew very little about.

Early on in this dating process, my wife and I received a phone call once again from my dad. He said that their old car had finally broken down, and it was going to be so expensive to fix that the mechanic said the car wasn't even worth fixing. He asked if there was anything we could possibly do to help. Not wanting to remind him that we had taken him a car and my stepmom refused to sit in it, I had to ask him, "What about Mom? Does she want me to buy another car? Because the last one I bought she wanted nothing to do with."

He said, "Well, she really doesn't have a choice unless she wants to walk because we have no other options."

I told my dad that I would discuss it with my wife and see what she wanted to do. The whole process of my wife's family having to go get the car and then bring it back to us in New Mexico did not go over well. After discussing it my wife said that if I wanted to take the money from the sale of the Cadillac and put it toward a different car, it was up to me. The truth was I was trying to do everything I could to achieve what the Bible said, which was that I am to honor my mother and father. Doing my best to walk in love to my dad, I decided to take the money from the sale of the previous car and go car shopping. We actually found a much newer car in good condition, and because we had already taken the time to drive the first car up there but could not spare that time again, we decided that when we bought it from the dealer, we would have them ship it to my dad and stepmom's house in the Midwest. This time they were appreciative.

My oldest daughter continued dating the same young man for quite some time, but since she was our first child to date, we were not really sure how to approach different problems that were starting to arise. We knew that she wanted to be around the young man, and in doing so she started attending his church instead of the church that we had been members of for her entire life. To make matters worse, she started questioning our belief in God because at this specific church, they felt that we were not serving God but that we were serving the devil. According to my daughter's new church, most churches were being demonically influenced, and with this information she became rebellious against our family and church. This whole process was not overnight; in fact, it took years for her to be persuaded that she had been taught wrong her entire life. My pastor has a saying that when Satan introduces you to ideas in your life, it's like putting a frog in a warm pot of water on the stove, and over a long period of time, slowly turning up the fire, hotter and hotter so that it doesn't even notice it's being cooked alive. My oldest daughter was being deceived slowly, and had decided that any words of wisdom that we had to give her were manifested by the devil and all we could do in her mind was tell her lies. Several months had passed, and my wife and I were coming to the end of our rope as to what we were to do about our oldest daughter. We were still running our business and managing our rental properties along with trying to keep up with school activities and after-school sports with my other two kids. More bad news was about to come.

It turned out that my stepmom was in the hospital dealing with an illness, and my dad was at the hospital every night visiting. One night he fell asleep, and when the nurse came in to check on my stepmother, she told him that he could not spend the night in the room, that he would have to leave and come back the next day. My dad told the nurse he was sorry and that he had intended to go home hours before but fell asleep by accident. He got into his car and started driving home. Somewhere along the trip to his house, he fell asleep and drove the car off the road into a ravine. They took him by ambulance to the hospital, and he was very badly beaten up, with several cuts and bruises, but he was alive. The doctors said that due to his age, the recovery process would not be easy, so when he was able, they moved him to a nursing home to further the recovery process. When he was told that his license to drive a car had been suspended and that it didn't look like he would ever get a driver's license issued to him again, he became very depressed. Over the coming months, his health continued to decline. I felt it was because he had lost his freedom. Now unable to drive and do things for himself, he was convinced that he had very little to look forward to. My wife and I asked if we could bring him out to New Mexico to stay with us like we had arranged for my mother to do, but separating my dad and my stepmom was not going to be possible, and there was no way in the world that she was ever going to agree to come out to New Mexico to stay with my wife and me. Because of this my dad had to stay in a nursing home with my stepmother in the Midwest.

The Passing of My Dad

Dealing with the spiritual battles that we were facing at home with my oldest daughter and the declining health of my dad had pushed my wife and me to our limits, but we knew that regardless of what the situation looked like, God was still in control. Every time I would call the nursing home and talk to my dad, his speech would to get worse and worse, and his ability to remember anything from one day to the next was diminishing as well. Sometimes he would even have trouble remembering my name, and talking to him became very difficult because he had trouble remembering who I was and just wanted to get off the phone. I chose to remember my dad as my coach, my childhood friend, and my fishing buddy, as well as the man who enjoyed watching race cars go around and around the track, constantly making left-hand turns. The man whom I was talking to now didn't really remember those things, and it was so incredibly painful to lose him. I prayed for him every day and just wanted to talk to him one more time with a clear mind like we used to do, but one day in October, I was notified by the nursing home that my dad had passed away. It was like watching a slow right hook coming at you; I knew it was coming, but when it landed, it still created a great deal of pain. The familiar pain of losing a parent was something that I had already experienced once, but my dad and I had a much different relationship than my mom. This was someone that I had millions of memories about, some funny and some sad and unfortunate, but a million memories all the same.

As my wife and I made plans for me to go back to the Midwest to help get things ready for his funeral, we decided that it would be best if I went by myself because of things that were going on with our business as well as problems that were taking place with my oldest daughter. As with all my kids, I had given my oldest daughter as much of my time growing up that was humanly possible, but somehow this had all been forgotten; all the memories that she had of growing up with her mother and me as well as her sister and brother had been forgotten. We had been replaced somehow with a new family and a different version of God that I didn't know. The church that she had been raised in as well as her family was now no longer needed. When I left to go help my family with my dad's funeral, my wife and I not only prayed for my family members who were grieving the loss, but we also prayed for my younger daughter and son that God would give them peace for the loss of their grandfather. We also lifted up my oldest daughter, that at some point in time, God would open her eyes and allow her to see things and also see how she had been deceived through these people who had been introduced into her life.

When I arrived in the Midwest, I stayed at a hotel room near my brother's house and together, we took care of most of the arrangements for our dad's funeral. On the morning that I was getting ready to go to the funeral, I received a phone call from my oldest daughter. The pastor at the new church that she had been attending with her boyfriend had decided to view the DVD that my pastor and I had made about my vision of heaven and hell. I could hear people in the background coaching my daughter as to what to say and how to ask questions. I thought she had called because she knew that I was going to my dad's funeral and wanted to say something concerning that. The thing that I know about the devil is that he knows when he can cause the most pain and exactly who to use to do it. And if that person is willing, then all I can do is withstand it and forgive. The people that were talking to her were oblivious to the fact that I was going to my dad's funeral, and she continued to ask me questions.

At different parts of the conversation, I could hear people in the background saying, "He's possessed of the devil" and "Listen to those demons trying to make excuses."

I said to my daughter, "Honey, I'm trying to get ready to go bury your grandfather. We probably need to talk about this some other time."

And in the background once again, I could hear them say, "Listen to him squirming; he doesn't want to talk about it because he is lying."

I was mad because of the insensitivity. I was crying because my oldest daughter was being used to carry out these callous acts by these people. To me she was just a tool to inflict pain on me as well as our family and our church.

I said to her, “I’m going to get off now because before long, I have to leave to go to the funeral home.”

In the background I could hear voices that were angry, telling her to keep asking questions, saying that I was lying. I hung up the phone and sat there on my bed in the hotel room by myself with my head in my hands and tears running down my forearms to my knees. I couldn’t believe my oldest daughter had been deceived by these hateful people who considered themselves godly.

My phone rang again, and it was my daughter once more. Trying to hold back the tears, I said, “I can’t do this right now; I need to go bury my father.”

I never did hear my daughter’s voice, but I could hear the angry people in the background saying different things, so again, I hung up the phone. I got myself back together and was able to get ready and go to my car. My phone rang once more, but this time I didn’t answer it; I just let it ring. I have endured a great deal of pain in my life, both physical and mental, but this was a whole different pain that had been inflicted on me. I was unsure of the long-term damage, but I knew the damage had been done. But now was not the time for that pain; it was time to refocus because I was about to lay eyes on my dad for the very last time until God calls me home to heaven.

Driving to the funeral home, a thousand different thoughts went through my mind. Why did I ever tell anyone that I could see into the spirit? When I was a kid, it only brought me problems because people thought I had mental issues, and now as an adult, it had created a great chasm between me and my oldest daughter, who was so incredibly precious to me. When I was on the phone, it was as if I could hear the demonic entities hissing and laughing about the damage that they had caused, about the pain they had inflicted between a father and a daughter.

Converging on the task at hand, I arrived at the funeral home, quickly dismissing my earlier thoughts and focusing now on my brothers, sisters, and family members who had come to pay their last respects to my dad. I knew that my dad had given his life to the Lord, and I had very little question where my father's final resting place in the universe would be. He was with the Lord. Funerals were always difficult for me, and not so much because you have to say goodbye to people in your life but because they expose spiritual strengths and weaknesses in the people who come to pay last respects. It allows people to look at themselves as human and mortal, that this time will come for each and every one of us, and it is times like this that each one of us has to reflect on where we will spend eternity. On each and every gravestone, there are three things: the day you were born, the day that you passed away and the dash in the middle that represents how you lived your life.

There were many tears and many hugs at my dad's funeral, but constantly in the back of my mind was the conversation that had taken place before I had arrived between my oldest daughter and myself. The one good thing about funerals is that you are able to reconnect with family members that you don't see often and visit with these people from your past who have come to pay their last respects. After taking care of the final details with my brother, we all said our goodbyes, and I started the long drive home by myself with my thoughts. I felt that I had kept secrets in my life from so many people and for so many years, secrets that if I had never told anyone, it would have been OK with me. Keeping secrets was something that I had always done incredibly well. These were things that on the trip home, I lifted up in prayer over and over, but my mind was clouded with so many different things—thoughts about my dad, thoughts about my oldest daughter and me; I was allowing this demon of deception to put a world of doubt in my mind.

When I returned home, all the quietness that was in my mind was replaced with the day-to-day chaos of running multiple businesses and being a husband and a dad. My oldest daughter's birthday was within a couple of weeks, and how this would play out was hard to tell. Due to the deception that was being played out in her life, my wife and I weren't even sure whether or not she would even want to celebrate the day with us. We bought birthday presents and cards just as if everything was normal, but all you had to do was ask my younger daughter and my son, and they would tell you that nothing was normal about the situation.

I had never known a group of people who called themselves godly and hated people around them so much. By this time, my oldest daughter was eating most of her meals with her boyfriend's family and church. The only thing she did at our house was go to bed and get up and go to school the next morning, using our car to take herself and her brother and sister to school. According to my other two kids, the ride on the way to school was all but silent; my oldest daughter would soon be seventeen years old and felt that she had acquired more than enough wisdom to make all life decisions on her own without any guidance from her mom and dad.

Defining Moment

At our church on Halloween, we would have an event for the kids to dress up in fun costumes and receive candy. On the day of the harvest party, we went to the church. As a general rule, my wife and I would volunteer to run some of the games, but this year we were unable to help because of some problems that came up with my oldest daughter. By this time we had attended the same church for nearly twenty years, and most of the congregation was like family to us, so informing some of our friends, we told them that we had some problems going on at home and would have to leave my daughter and son to stay at the church and play games. When my wife and I arrived at our house, there was no one there, but just after the sun went down, a car showed up at the house. In the car was our oldest daughter and her boyfriend, and demonic entities were moving about randomly. My daughter proceeded to inform my wife and me that she no longer had to obey us because the people at the other church convinced her we were evil. The young man I spoke of earlier, who lived on the property in one of the rental houses, came out to see what was happening. He did his best to try and calm down my oldest daughter. As I said before, he was like a son to my wife and me and a brother to my kids, so this scene was very painful for him as well. The young man and my wife stayed in the front yard to try to talk sense into my oldest daughter, but she was already deceived to the point that she felt as if the only people she could trust were the same people who were tearing her away from her family. My wife then proceeded to tell her that if she could no longer abide by our rules, then she could no longer live at our house. She was going to be moving out on the day before her seventeenth birthday. I don't believe she had been expecting this. She believed that she could continue to live in our house, manipulating and tormenting her siblings and us because they had convinced her that this was the right thing to do.

At this point law enforcement was contacted, and they informed my wife that if my daughter had a safe place to go, she could proceed to leave with as many belongings as she could carry because she was of age. My daughter contacted her "new family," and they came to pick her up with her belongings. The young man who was like my daughter's brother accompanied my wife and daughter to her room to pack up her things. It was not a pleasant moment, and he was baffled at the way my daughter was treating my wife; he tried to correct her in an attempt to protect my wife from the barrage of verbal communication from my daughter. I think at that moment is when the level of deception was finally realized by all of us, family or not.

My daughter went in and out of the house repeatedly so that she could move as many of her things out of the house as possible; she felt as if we would damage her possessions or destroy them. We asked, "Why in the world would we do that?"

What I remember most about that night was how incredibly hateful and angry these people were. I felt as if they were dragging the demonic entities that were fueling this fire in and out of my house as well. When as much as possible had been moved for that night and my wife and I were mentally exhausted, we also gave our daughter her birthday gifts to take with her because we were not going to be welcome at her seventeenth birthday.

My wife and I were angry and frustrated that this was actually happening. We called our friends at the church and asked them to go ahead and bring our youngest daughter and son to the house when the harvest party was over because we were not going to be able to go back to pick them up due to the circumstances. As my other two kids arrived at the house, my oldest daughter and her entourage were leaving. The other two kids didn't have any idea what was going on, and at first they cried because they were losing their sister. The young man who lived on the property, my wife, my youngest daughter and son, and I sat dazed in our living room, trying to figure out what just happened and do our best to console each other. The demonic entities that had earlier invaded our home were still present and were doing their best to try and cause confusion and pain within the confines of our mind. Over and over, I would cast them out in Jesus's name, but this was a wound that was not easily healed. I knew in my heart that it would take time to put the pieces of our family back together again. As for my younger daughter and son, they were partly relieved because of the pressure that had been constantly present in our home. Later on, they revealed that there were times when their older sister was home that they felt as if they were in some sort of danger, and now that the weight had been removed, they were sleeping better than they had in quite some time.

I continued to question myself, wondering if I had never revealed my gift of seeing in the spirit, whether this conclusion with my daughter may have been diverted. I had been deceived before as well by the demonic spirit of deception, but at this point in my life, I had recently lost my father and now seemingly was losing my oldest daughter, and I felt like I was to blame.

All three of my kids attended the same school, and this made things extremely difficult for my youngest daughter and son because on occasion, they would see their older sister in the school, and she had made the decision to completely ignore her brother and sister. Because my wife was still in the military and was often unable to go to school events, I was the one who went to most of the parent-teacher conferences as well as the sporting events, and it was very painful for me as well. Most of the time, when I would see my oldest daughter in the hallways, she would either avoid me or ignore me, and I'm sure in some ways she wished that I didn't exist. As a father I played back my oldest daughter's childhood again and again to try to figure out where it was exactly that I started doing things wrong. It was the same old adage of the frog in the boiling water. Once my oldest daughter started going off the path and in the wrong direction, it began to spiral out of control. But as a parent, I continued to blame myself because I didn't catch it sooner and redirect her on the right path. She was my oldest and my first, and my wife and I were not about to make the same mistakes with our other two kids. My wife and I did everything we could do within our power. We asked God to protect her and keep her safe. We prayed in Jesus's name that she would be restored and brought back to us. All we wanted was our daughter back and to be a family again. Amen.

Chapter 15: Forgiveness and Restoration

It had been a difficult year for our family. We had endured and been put through far more than we had anticipated, but we did our best to pick up the pieces and continue on as the very close family that we were. This was the new normal for us, and when the end of the year came around, our prayer was that the following year was going to be much better than the previous. But what we received in the early part of that next year was that my oldest daughter and her boyfriend were going to be married during the summer break before her senior year. We didn't know what this meant because we had assumed that we would play a very small part of the wedding—if we were going to be invited at all. As much as the people in this congregation disliked other churches, my family, and me, we had been informed that our presence had been requested. The thought of being around this group of people, who had entered my house, bringing their demonic entities with them to impose their dark faith upon my household, was not something that anyone in our family had looked forward to. But the healing process had to begin, and we as a family decided that we were going to forgive and not hold any grudges toward the people in this congregation, as well as my daughter and her future husband.

Sometimes forgiving people hurts, and I know that our Lord and Savior understands this unconditionally. We all understand that the word says that if we are to be forgiven, then we must first forgive. I can only speak for myself, but when the day of my oldest daughter's wedding arrived, it was all I could do to even show up. Very few people even said a word to us, and it was decided that my wife was to walk up with the young man's mother and light a candle. I was asked to walk my daughter down the aisle. My stomach was in knots, and I tried everything I could think of to not show the mental pain that I was in; every part of me just wanted to get this over with and get this whole thing behind us. Not because I was losing a daughter and gaining a son-in-law, but because there was so much hatred in this building toward me and my family that I felt like I just wanted to get them to safety. During the service it wasn't like I could see in the spirit the demonic entities moving about the building; it was more like I could sense them and their presence. Under my breath I prayed a hedge of protection around my family members and myself. My pastor from our church and his wife came to the wedding with a few of our closest friends. I think they felt that my wife and I needed at least a few allies in this building.

At the dinner after the wedding, the bride and groom, along with the family of the groom, sat at the head table, but there were no seats for my wife and me and our kids. We were told to sit with all of the other invited guests. My wife and I were trying our best to act as if everything was normal, but the truth was it wasn't normal at all. We knew that my daughter had been deceived and that she was getting married way too young—a life mistake that we knew at some point in time was going to cost her. But we hoped for the best and believed that in time God would open their eyes and allow them to see things clearly.

The day of my oldest daughter's wedding had physically made me sick. Once again I questioned myself about decisions I had made, as well as things I had allowed to take place. I know that sometimes when we are traveling through the valley of the shadow of death, we question ourselves and decisions that we have made, and I always returned to the same conclusion: that if I had never allowed people to know that I had been given the gift of seeing into the supernatural realm, it was possible that this may have never happened.

I became quietly depressed, not really letting anyone know the feelings that were welling up inside me. I knew better, but I was letting this demonic entity of deception have a foothold within the confines of my mind. I wish that I could say that I bounced back like a mighty man of God, but at this time in my life, I felt anything but mighty. I knew that for my youngest daughter, my son, and especially my wife, I needed to act my way into feeling like I was a useful part of the kingdom of God once again.

That year when I was to attend our annual men's advance, I needed to heal. Most of the time when I would attend these events, I was the one doing the ministering. At this particular event, I was the one that the ministering angels were following around. I wasn't one who broke under the spirit at the drop of a hat, but at this particular event, I found myself crying like a baby. The words that kept coming to me in the spirit were that sometimes you need to mourn, and this was my time to mourn and heal and then return to my post stronger than before. Whether the pastors whom I was constantly surrounded by at these men's events knew it or not, by me sharing what I was seeing in the spirit was simultaneously healing me of an emotional pain that was like no other physical pain I had experienced in my life. At first, I was a little quieter than usual around the pastors and the other men at the event, but the truth was that I didn't talk that much anyway. I tried to listen and observe and speak when it was relevant. I am sure that even my closest friends were aware of the spiritual battle that was going on inside of me, and as always, I knew that I was fighting this battle from a place of victory through Christ Jesus.

It was at this men's event that I was able to rid myself of the heavy burden that manifested as self-doubt and also to forgive my daughter and the people whom she had surrounded herself with and to bind the demons of deception that had caused all this pain. Forgiveness is a powerful weapon. I knew without a doubt that this was a spiritual battle being fought, not one of flesh and blood. I knew the weapons that I needed to overcome this were his word, prayer, and fasting. As the event went on and the pastors would ask me questions, I once again felt like a commentator at a football game, describing what was happening on the field almost as if they were experiencing the game on the radio back in the early twentieth century. What I found out was that this symbiotic relationship that I had with the pastors was actually refocusing me. I needed to be in the presence of God, helping my brothers in Christ to move forward in their lives and, in turn, restoring mine.

Focusing on the Day to Day

Once we came home after the men's advance, it was easy to lose myself in the affairs of my life. Sometimes busy is good; it doesn't allow the enemy to input things into our mind. By this time, our business had grown, and even our competitors across town who had reopened under a new name were once again going to shut down. The angel that had appeared to me on what was now hole one of the miniature golf course had said that once we had defeated our Goliath, in time there would be no trace of the former business. We had also built a paintball field as well as a bumper-boat pond for a variety of attractions at the park. We still had several rental properties and my wife's military career as well. There were always baseball games, basketball games, and football games to attend with my younger daughter and son. God had blessed us with an incredible life, but we were extraordinarily busy as well.

Quietly my wife and I continued to battle, sometimes day by day, and when thoughts would enter my mind, it became easier to dismiss them, binding the demons of deception and casting them out in Jesus's name. It says in 2 Corinthians 10:5 (NLT), "And we take captive every thought to make it obedient to Christ." Keeping things to myself was almost as easy as breathing. My wife and I continued on and began the work of putting the pieces of our life back together. We realized that helping people past the mountains they were facing in their lives allowed us to heal in ours as well. Many people looked at my family and were sure that we had this amazing life and would speak over us saying things like, "It must be nice to be so blessed."

Like the verse says in Luke 6:38 (NLT), "Give, and it will be given to you, good measure, pressed down, shaken together and running over, will be poured into your lap. For with the measure you use, it will be measured to you." And as our friends and loved ones spoke over us, my wife and I would receive every word and knew that in time what had been spoken over us for so long would manifest in the natural and allow us to be a blessing to the kingdom of God and the body of Christ. What people didn't know was that every time that we opened the gates to our business, we were sacrificing ourselves as servants to this community and the surrounding area. We did everything within our power to make sure that we created good memories that would last generations for the families that patronized our facility. What I found out, over and over again, was that the word of God was proven true, as in Matthew 6:4, NIV: "So that your giving may be in secret. Then your father, who sees what is done in secret, will reward you openly."

In time everything that had been spoken over us for more than a decade would begin to come to pass. My wife and I would begin to experience things in our Christian walk that we never thought possible: a ministry, financial blessings being poured out, and the ability to affect different countries around the world. My oldest daughter came full circle and rededicated her life to the Lord and became a blessing to many young adults, making them aware of the snares that the darkness of this world would set and helping them to avoid these pitfalls. She remarried, this time to a godly man who can lead her, and together they are equally yoked. I have no doubt that together they will make an impact for the body of Christ.

My youngest daughter decided to follow in the footsteps of her grandparents and her mother and father by serving her country in the military. She and her husband have made my wife and me so proud to call her our daughter, and only God knows what they will achieve in the coming years. We know there is a special blessing on her and the presence of God that surrounds her and her family.

As for my son, he is a mighty man of God. I have never known a young man who put so much effort into being a devout witness, a testimony, and a light to the world that has been placed on a hill for all to see. He is everything in the world that I wish that I could have been at his age. His faith in God rivals that of many righteous men more than twice his age. God knows what lies before him in the pages of his book, but whatever it is, it will be incredible, and the joy of my heart is to see it play out.

But all these things I am mentioning are pages of a book that has not been written. It is a testimony, a glance into a part of my life that has not yet been told. God has blessed me with a life rich in health, spiritual prosperity, wisdom, knowledge, insight, and favor. My gift once again flows from a place of victory in Christ Jesus. My wife and I spent many years sowing into people's lives as well as our children and family members, and like a good farmer who reaps a bountiful crop from the good seeds that he has sown, we now live in a place of abundance in all aspects of our life.

I have come to an understanding that I have an assignment in the body of Christ and the kingdom of God, and I know that only through my trust in him are all things possible. Regardless of what you have been through in your life, our God is a God of restoration and we all have a valuable position to fill in the body of Christ.

ACKNOWLEDGMENTS

I give special thanks to the pastors whom God has used to teach me the word and show me that we can still be true to who we are as men: Pastor David Swann and family, Pastor Rick Raney, Pastor Stormy Swann, Pastor Troy Smothermon, Pastor Rick Burke, and Pastor Steve Smothermon. An additional thank-you goes to my friends who have always been there for me: the Lofton family, the Drake family, the Thompson family, the Sackreiter family, Rusty Foreman, and John Butts (J. B.). Thanks to my wife, Kara, for her editing, Jamie Garcia for editing, Cole Henry for the book cover graphic, Bailey Thompson-Garcia for book cover design, and Alexandra Moreno for artwork.

Anyone who thinks that life is a solo act is sorely wrong. Thank you to everyone who has contributed to my life, good or bad; I learned from both.

Made in USA - Kendallville, IN
1170350_9781733696050
09.25.2020 0842